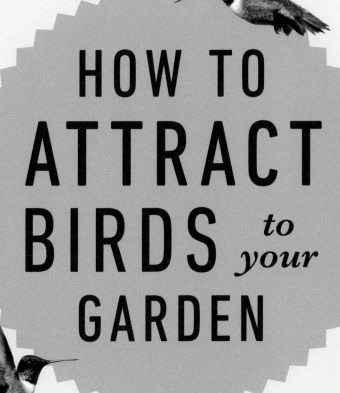

HOW TO ATTRACT BIRDS *to your* GARDEN

DAN ROUSE

CONTENTS

INTRODUCTION

*Birds share our world. For me they have been,
and will always be, a vital part of my life.*

Since the age of four, I have loved birds. It all began when we created a bird feeding box to go onto the garden wall. Our family home is near a park with plenty of trees nearby and the number of birds in the garden always fascinated me. The feeding box brought in even more birds, and I started to notice details about them and their habits. The same feeding box is still alive and well-ish on the wall in the garden and continues to attract house sparrows and starlings.

My parents, especially my dad, have always encouraged my obsession with birds and the natural world, allowing me to take over the garden with my creations, filling every corner with a nest box or feeding station of some kind. Since childhood I have taken my binoculars and bird-spotting book with me on every family holiday and day trip. My love for birds has increased as I find out more about them, and I now try to encourage others to appreciate birds as much as I do.

With many species declining due to lack of space and nesting opportunities, it's vitally important that we now take birds into our lives, and the garden is the best place to start. Birds don't care whether you live in a flat with a balcony, in a busy street, or in a house with acres of land; everyone can attract birds to their outdoor space as I have done. In the first chapter of this book you will find basic information on birds' lives and behavior. There follow chapters on feeding, nesting, planting for birds, adding water to your outdoor space, and keeping birds safe. At the end of the book are profiles of 56 birds you may see in your garden. Some birds are so familiar that we hardly notice them, but all have their own habits and traits. I hope that by starting to adapt your garden for birds you will gain a greater appreciation and enjoyment of every type of bird, and that your garden will be filled with life and interest all year round.

Bird feeders are a simple and effective way to start bringing more birds to your garden. You can make your own feeders and mix your own food.

BIRD BEHAVIOR

BIRD
BEHAVIOR

Your yard can feel like a different place when you share it with birds. You become more aware of the distinctive movements of certain birds around the yard. You build up a picture of what the seasons mean for birds, and what their habits are through the year, from nesting and rearing their young, to foraging for food.

Hummingbirds are common in backyards, attracted by colorful, nectar-rich blossoms in spring and summer, as well as special nectar feeders.

BIRDS IN YOUR YARD

Endlessly fascinating, birds bring movement, color, and their distinctive songs and calls to your yard.

Yards are more important than ever to many common birds. Most birds that visit yards come from farmland or woodland. These birds are now declining as farmland is worked more intensively, and agricultural land is built upon, so they have come to rely on yards for what they need. You can attract more birds to your yard, including some less common ones, by providing the right food and nesting conditions, plants for food and shelter, and a good source of water.

A feeding station offers a choice for different birds, with special seeds for some species such as goldfinches, alongside others that are popular with a number of species. The combination will draw birds into the yard.

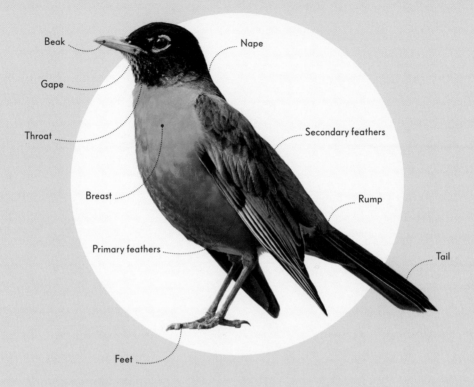

Beak

Gape

Throat

Breast

Primary feathers

Feet

Nape

Secondary feathers

Rump

Tail

Birds are light and streamlined so they can fly efficiently. Knowing the parts of the body and areas of markings helps you pinpoint and describe the features you see more accurately.

Birds play a key part in the ecology of your yard and its surroundings: from eating aphids, caterpillars, and snails, to distributing seeds from trees and other plants. This is true for any outdoor space: birds will come and feed in a courtyard or visit a balcony.

You don't need to know much about birds to enjoy seeing them in your yard, but you may want to start to find out more as you see them up close. Learning the basics of identification helps you know which birds are visiting your yard. The size, shape, and colors allow you to narrow down which type of bird it is. If you can

become familiar with the names for different parts of a bird's body (above), this will make it easier for you to look it up (*see pp.158–185*) or compare it to other similar birds. Over time, you can also tune into the calls and songs of different birds, their movement and shape in flight, and where you are likely to see them. Some are shy and stay close to the ground, others are very active and flit from tree to tree, while others perch up high, and rarely venture into a yard. Once you know the birds that commonly visit your yard, you will notice and start to look forward to seeing unusual or seasonal visitors.

In the canopy
Agile warblers and sparrows quickly move around the canopy where they are less of a target for predators. In spring and summer, the foliage is dense; in fall and winter there are enough twigs to stop aerial predators.

On trees
Many birds, including blue jays, perch high up as a vantage point. Brown creepers' patterned plumage is the perfect camouflage, allowing them to scale trees unnoticed.

Yellow warbler

American robin

On the ground
Quite large birds such as thrushes, crows, and doves spend their time on the ground, often flying to and from perches. Much smaller birds such as wrens and sparrows also hop among shrubs and bushes on the ground, their muted colors making them less visible.

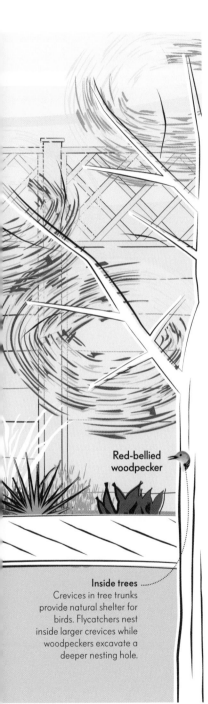

Red-bellied woodpecker

Inside trees
Crevices in tree trunks provide natural shelter for birds. Flycatchers nest inside larger crevices while woodpeckers excavate a deeper nesting hole.

HOW BIRDS BEHAVE AND INTERACT

Birds feed and nest in a huge range of areas, so diverse habitats are the key to attracting a variety of birds.

Birds have different habits and needs, which means that many can coexist in the same space. Being able to feed safely is vital, and different species feed in different areas, depending on what they eat and their size. They may also spend time looking for nesting materials and building a nest for breeding. Some birds are territorial, especially in the breeding season, defending their turf from others, often by singing or directly chasing the competition away.

In the ideal bird-friendly yard (*see pp.98–99*), you will have areas of shrubs and bushes where shier species, such as wrens, can stay, appearing only to make a dash for food. Trees are used in many ways by different birds. Some nest there or feed on insects or seeds, or shelter their young and themselves. You can create a similar sheltered habitat with climbing plants on walls or fences. Some ground space benefits birds such as thrushes, which often use low-growing or container plants to hide in when startled, before returning to their feeding or nesting sites. Nest boxes or roosting baskets (*see pp.78–79*) can supplement the natural shelter your yard offers.

A mix of container plants and low shrubs provides shelter for ground-feeding birds, while shrubs and trees offer higher points for birds to perch and nest.

HOW BIRDS FEED AND FORAGE

A bird's body structure, diet, feet, and type of beak affect where they look for their ideal meal.

Birds need to feed often on nutritious foods to give them the energy they need. If you want to influence which birds come into your yard, and attract more of them, you can increase the range of options available for them to feed by enriching several natural habitats *(see pp.98–119)*. There are four main areas in the yard where birds naturally feed.

On the ground

Larger birds that eat insects and worms feed on the ground, as do scavengers such as crows, gulls, and pigeons. In yards there are often spillages of food on the ground from feeders, which attract more birds.

Ground-feeding species include:
American robin, northern mockingbird, wood thrush, Swainson's thrush, hermit thrush, common grackle, mourning dove, American crow, black-billed magpie, and herring gull.

Robins primarily feed on the ground as they look for worms and other invertebrates as well as fallen food.

On trees

Trees are an essential source of seeds and fruit as well as insects and larvae. Many birds rely on food they can find in bark and on leaves—even seed eaters such as sparrows need caterpillars for their chicks.

Birds that feed on trees include: red-bellied woodpecker, downy woodpecker, pileated woodpecker, brown creeper, warblers, and kinglets.

Woodpeckers (including the red-bellied woodpecker, *left*) and brown creepers use their long, slender beaks to probe cracks in bark for insects.

In trees

Some birds collect nuts and larger pieces of food and cache them in tree cavities during the colder months in particular. These birds are pretty feisty and defend their territories to protect their caches.

Birds that store food in trees include: nuthatches, chickadees, and jays.

Chickadees hide seeds and nuts in tree crevices for later retrieval.

In shrubs and low plants

Flowers and shrubs are ideal small spaces for foraging. Some birds rely on this cover for security as they feed.

Birds that feed in low plants include: gray catbird, black-and-white warblers, yellow-rumped warbler, Carolina wren, house wren.

Wrens stay in shrubs and flower beds to avoid predators and feed on insects that live in dark, damp spots.

WHERE BIRDS NEST

*All birds need a safe place to rear their young,
and they choose their nesting spot carefully.*

Nests are not homes for birds, but seasonal places built to lay eggs and raise chicks. Some birds nest high off the ground using various strategies to fend off predators, such as living in colonies. Others nest near ground level and vigorously defend their nest, often with the male chasing away other birds. Nocturnal birds nest where they feel protected during the day as they roost, such as in nest boxes and tree cavities. A few birds build nests on buildings and sheds.

Mourning dove

In shrubs

Birds such as thrushes typically nest in shrubs or hedges where they have some protection and security for laying eggs and raising their young. Brown thrashers also create their nests in shrubs, forming a perfectly round nest attached to branches and twigs to keep it safe.
Birds that nest in shrubs include: Swainson's thrush, gray catbird, red-winged blackbird, northern cardinal.

Blackbirds use materials such as twigs, moss, and foliage found within yards to weave a bowl-shaped nest, then line it with grasses.

In the open

Birds can avoid ground predators by nesting further up trees, shrubs, and hedges. These nests give birds a good vantage point to keep a look out for potential danger. Larger birds such as pigeons and doves position their nests out in the open. Finches make their nests on the ends of branches, using twigs and moss often stuck together using spiders' silk.
Birds that nest in the open include: purple finch, house finch, pine siskin, American goldfinch, mourning dove.

Mourning doves make loose nests of twigs, grass, and weeds on branches that may be seen through from below.

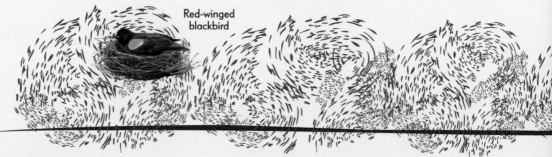

Red-winged blackbird

Black-billed
magpie

High up

The higher the nest, the more of an advantage
a bird has over its ground predators, though it
may be vulnerable from above. Some crow
family members (known as corvids) create
their nests high in trees, roosting and nesting
in groups to give them protection in numbers.
Birds that nest high up include: American
crows, black-billed magpies.

**Magpies, unlike jays and crows,
do not nest in groups.**

Eastern
screech owl

In holes

Some birds, like woodpeckers, nest in holes in tree
trunks that they created. Other birds, unable to make
their own, use cavities abandoned by woodpeckers,
other natural cavities, or nest boxes. Red-breasted
nuthatches apply sticky conifer pitch to the entrance
of the nest hole to deter predators.
Birds that nest in holes include: woodpeckers,
nuthatches, chickadees, bluebirds, tree swallows, wood
ducks, and American kestrels.

**Eastern screech owls nest in enlarged natural
cavities in deciduous trees. They usually roost
in tree holes or dense foliage during the day.**

RAISING YOUNG BIRDS

Many birds breed in and around yards using natural or artificial nesting sites, and they also bring their young in search of food.

At breeding time, it's fascinating to see juvenile (young) birds and how they interact with their parents. Many juveniles have a similar plumage to the adults but are duller until they molt into adult-type feathers in the fall following fledging. The duller plumage acts as camouflage. Some juveniles are more different from their parents. Young robins, for example, have no red on the breast, reducing their visibility to predators, and preventing adult robins from chasing them away. Young starlings are dull brown instead of the glossy, metallic black of their parents.

Many juvenile birds have a bright yellow interior to their mouths, known as a gape. They retain this yellow coloring for some time after they leave the nest, and the gape flanges—the edges visible when the beak is closed—can be a useful way to identify a young bird.

Behavior is another way to identify young birds. They often sit in a secure spot waiting for their parents to bring them food. When an adult approaches, they squat and shake their wings with their mouths wide open showing their gape. They also make a high-pitched noise from the nest when competing for attention and food.

Young birds in the nest open their beaks wide, showing their bright gapes, making their beaks an easy "target" for parents. In some species, the coloration of their gapes is on the ultraviolet (UV) spectrum, visible in dim light inside cavities.

Nestlings often peer out of the nest when they hear an adult approaching. Typically they make a high-pitched noise and compete for the attention of the adult to be fed first.

WHAT TO DO IF YOU FIND A YOUNG BIRD

The best advice in nearly all cases is to leave it alone and move away from any young bird that you find, and the adult will return. The parent may be nearby but waiting for you to leave. If you are concerned about predation, or if the bird is on a road or sidewalk where it might be injured, provide the bird with some shelter such as a box, or move it to a safer place as near as possible to where you found it. If no adults return within a few hours, contact your local bird or animal rescue center.

The adult chipping sparrow brings small pieces of food to place into the young bird's mouth. The young bird squats down to take the food.

RESIDENT BACKYARD BIRDS

Many birds live, feed, and breed in the same small area for their whole life. These are the ones most likely to visit your yard.

Regular backyard visitors become a familiar sight as they share your outdoor space. Watching these birds as they feed and shelter in your yard gives you an unrivaled opportunity to get to know their habits and interactions, as well as which parts of the yard each type of bird prefers. If you add more features to attract birds, from feeders to a birdbath, to more wildlife-friendly plantings, you will see bird numbers and activity increase in your area.

American robin

Considered widely as the "harbinger of spring," robins are probably the most recognizable of backyard birds, with their red breast and habit of hopping, then pausing on lawns to capture an earthworm out of the ground. They are very territorial, having their own areas for breeding and feeding, and defending their turf fiercely against other birds (*see also p.166*).

American goldfinch

These colorful birds often arrive in a noisy flock, known as a charm of goldfinches. Often other finches, such as pine siskins and common redpolls flock with them, especially over the winter. They are drawn to feeders, particularly if you provide niger seed (*see also p.183*).

Tufted titmouse

This perky gray bird with its bushy crest whistles a sprightly "peter peter peter" song nearly year-round. They have been known to pluck hair from live mammals to line their nests. Also, when they are perched on trays containing sunflower seeds, they commonly take the largest seed and fly away to a perch to crack it open with their stout bill (*see also p.174*).

House wren

House wrens can be seen from farms to city centers and love to live near people. A gardener's helper, they actively search for insects. They are energetic, vibrant singers that nest in nest boxes provided, or a variety of other cavities such as flowerpots, boots, or mailboxes (*see also p.164*).

Baltimore oriole

The sighting of the brilliant orange plumage of the male Baltimore oriole should be a visual reminder to bird lovers to offer these wonderful guests cut orange halves in feeders. Once the leaves come out on the trees, these birds will be heard—by their rich, whistling song while foraging for insects high in the canopy—more often than seen (see also p.179).

Northern mockingbird

The beauty of this bird's voice and song repertoire once played a role in the capture and sale of this species as a house pet in the 19th century. Fortunately, that practice has been outlawed and this proud and flashy bird once again sings in its natural habitat and is very common in towns and cities (see also p.176).

Chipping sparrow

The chipping sparrow is a crisp-looking small bird with a bright rusty cap, found in yards throughout much of the country. In earlier times, it was well known for using horsehair to line its nests. During the summer, you can hear the male's distinctive long, buzzy trill in branches of a nearby tree (*see also p.181*).

House finch

House finches are another regular backyard visitor. Being highly social, they are often seen together in groups. They are quite vocal and may be heard singing any time of the year in a high perch. Male house finches and purple finches look quite similar and require careful viewing to distinguish them from each other (*see also p.183*).

SPRING AND SUMMER VISITORS

Migrating birds arrive from warmer areas to feast on the abundant food in yards.

Birds that are resident all year are joined by those on migration. Migrants often return to the same area, and even the same nest, year after year. These visitors can be a seasonal highlight and they are seen by many as heralding the arrival of summer. They will spend the spring and summer months building nests, breeding, feeding, and raising the next generation.

Barn swallow

Wintering in South America, barn swallows begin their journey north in February, spreading out over much of North America by May. They feed on insects over water and fields before creating cuplike nests on structures with easy access, such as eaves of houses (*see also p.163*).

Yellow warbler

These bright yellow birds breed across the mid and central states in the US, making pit stops in the southern regions before wintering in Central America and the northern part of South America. They are one of the first warblers to make their summer and winter migrations (*see also p.170*).

OTHER SUMMERING BIRDS:

- Baltimore oriole
- Brown-headed cowbirds
- Chipping sparrow
- Song sparrow
- American tree sparrow
- Red-winged blackbird
- Swainson's thrush
- Veery
- Gray catbird
- Chimney swift
- Ruby-throated hummingbird
- American redstart
- Yellow-rumped warbler

Purple martin

Traveling from the warm tropics of the Amazon basin in the winter, to the warmer climates of the mid and eastern states in the US, this agile flyer is one of the first summer migrants to arrive. They nest in the eaves of houses and cavities in trees in small colonies, and readily take to artificial nest sites , nesting close to humans during their summer stay (*see also p.164*).

Scarlet tanager

Another long-distance migrant, these birds breed in the eastern regions of North America and winter in South America. This is a species that migrates at night. Birds that migrate further south in South America return to their breeding grounds in synchronized bursts and later than those birds that winter further north in South America (*see also p.172*).

FALL AND
WINTER VISITORS

*In the colder months, migrants look for food
and warmth, frequently visiting bird feeders.*

During the fall and winter months, birds such as waxwings and some types of finches migrate south from their northern breeding grounds to escape the harsh weather and live where food is more readily available, often near yards. They group together into flocks and form very active, and sometimes noisy, gatherings. Smaller birds may often flit from yard to yard in groups, visiting feeders, and huddling together during the night for warmth.

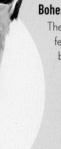

Bohemian waxwing
These beautifully colored birds with striking facial features form large flocks that roam south from their breeding grounds across the northern US and Canada in search of fruit. They are attracted to trees with fruits and berries, and usually descend on crab apple, cherry, and plum trees in town, and berries of mountain ash in yards (*see also p.165*).

Dark-eyed junco
The majority of these birds return from their breeding grounds in the colder climates of Canada and Alaska to the southern parts of the US. They are found in flocks around the edges of woods or suburban yards looking for grass or weed seeds on the ground and flying into nearby bushes when threatened (*see also p.180*).

OTHER WINTERING BIRDS

- Red crossbill
- Snow bunting
- Cedar waxwing
- Evening grosbeak
- Common redpoll
- White-winged crossbill
- Pine siskin
- Red-breasted nuthatch
- Golden-crowned kinglet
- Yellow-rumped warbler

White-throated sparrow

These sparrows are found in small pockets in the northeast throughout the year. Many migrate from northern regions to the southern states for the winter and search for weed and grass seeds. They will take millet and black oil sunflower seeds from feeders placed near sheltering bushes (*see also p.182*).

American tree sparrow

These tiny little birds breed in the northernmost part of North America before making their way down to the center of the continent. These birds migrate in flocks during the night, and females typically winter further south than males (*see also p.180*).

BACKYARD FEATURES FOR BIRDS

To attract birds into your yard,
boost the four essentials: food, nesting sites,
plants for shelter, and water.

A combination of readily available food, the right nesting conditions, plants for cover, and water for drinking and bathing allows birds to visit your yard all year. The yard will also provide a good stop for migratory birds that arrive to breed, or come in the winter to feed.

Eastern bluebirds catch insects to feed to their young, but also like berries, dried fruit, or mealworms placed on a tray type feeder.

Food

Birds will eat whatever is easiest to obtain, whether it's from natural sources, such as insects from a pond or on plants, or from feeders that you provide, or often a combination of both. Adapt the food you put out to suit how different species feed, the birds' activities through the year, and the changing seasons. Some birds, such as jays, crows, and doves, are willing to feed on just about anything. Others have a distinct preference as to what food they like and can access, as well as what is best for carrying and feeding to their young. Seasonal visitors may benefit from food that contains a high amount of fat to give them energy before their migration or replenish their reserves afterward. Experiment with different places to put bird feeders in your yard and what types of food to provide at different times of the year, and make sure to take precautions to discourage predators (see also pp.148–149).

Nesting

There are many ways to provide a good nesting habitat, from choosing plants that offer shelter and a safe environment, to putting up a particular nest box, whether homemade or purchased specially to suit a certain species. Be aware of the nesting potential in your area, including high trees, houses or buildings, and hedges or ground-level plants. Nest box design, size, and location play a key part in attracting the right birds. Leaving out nesting materials for birds to gather is also helpful (see also pp.90–91). Catering for all the species that you see in your yard is nearly impossible unless you have a vast amount of land, because many birds are territorial and require a certain distance between their nest and those of other territorial birds.

Female house wrens choose one nest among many a male builds. While often using nest boxes, her choice can be eccentric: a boot, flower pot, or small can.

Red-eyed vireos' nests are concealed by foliage above and suspended from a tree branch away from the trunk to give a panoramic view of the surroundings.

Plants

As the element in the yard that binds all the other features together, plants can meet many of the needs of birds. Flowers attract insects for birds to feed on, and provide nectar and pollen that some birds love to eat directly. Dense branches and foliage of shrubs, trees, and climbing plants are places for birds to roost or breed and find sanctuary between feeding and nesting. Trees in or near your yard can provide a source of food, from insects to fruit and berries, particularly during the winter when other resources are scarce. Plants can also provide water for birds, with leaves collecting moisture and fruits containing water. Every outdoor space, from courtyards and balconies to larger yards, can be a home to a collection of varied and beautiful plants that will be useful to birds (*see also pp.98–119*).

Look for northern mockingbirds in berry bushes any time of the year. In summer, they add a variety of insects to their diet.

The tufted titmouse forages for insects, and often takes seed to hide in bark crevices or in the ground.

Water

Water is vital to create the ideal yard for birds. A water source is a place for drinking: some birds drink from dew drops on plants or obtain moisture from the food they eat, but for the most part they need an area where they can regularly drink. Water also provides a habitat for the prey of some birds. Some owls, for example, seek frogs or toads as prey items, or plunge down to catch small mammals that are using the water as a place to groom. Other species such as swallows feed on insects and other invertebrates that use the water to breed, swooping down and picking them off the surface. Having water sources in your yard, such as birdbaths or ponds, gives birds a safe place to bathe. This

With her nest near water, this common grackle female is taking time out for a drink and a bath.

keeps the birds in good condition—particularly their feathers—as regular bathing helps them remove any harmful buildup of parasites and bacteria (see also pp.126–127).

Northern cardinals love water for bathing and drinking. Add a heated birdbath to your yard if you live where water freezes in the winter.

FEEDING
BIRDS

FEEDING BIRDS

The simplest way to attract birds to your yard is by putting up a bird feeder. With a little knowledge about the types of food and feeders available, you can create a feeding station that will appeal to a variety of species. Once birds discover the food is there (often surprisingly quickly), they will keep coming back for more.

American goldfinches are some of the most entertaining backyard visitors to watch as they dart to and fro. Here, they are feeding energetically on niger seeds.

FOOT TYPE
AND FEEDING

Looking at birds' feet gives you an insight into how they move and feed. Their feet determine which bird feeders they can access.

Body size and shape affect how birds feed and their agility, but their feet, which are adapted to their natural habitats, play a huge part in enabling them to access certain foods.

Most common backyard birds can be gathered into four different groups based on the way their claws and feet are structured: long claws, flat feet, woodpecker feet, and raptor feet.

Brown creeper

Long claws
allow birds to grip and maneuver easily.

Long claws

Many smaller birds have slender feet with three long toes pointing forward and one hindclaw pointing backward. Each toe has a long, curved claw. Their feet give a good all-around ability to perch, hop, or walk. They have a strong grip on small twigs, so ruby-crowned kinglets and Carolina chickadees, for example, can feed acrobatically, even hanging upside down. Brown creepers have an excellent grip on tree bark but are not able to walk on the ground. These feet are not used to catch or carry prey or other items. Long-clawed birds can access many types of feeder.

Species include: brown creeper, Carolina chickadee, chestnut-backed chickadee, white-breasted nuthatch, scarlet tanager, red-eyed vireo, yellow-rumped warbler, black-and-white warbler, ruby-crowned kinglet.

Woodpecker feet

Woodpeckers have two toes pointing forward and two pointing backward. The outer toe is long and reversed, giving a good grip on rounded branches, although the tail is also needed as a support. Woodpeckers typically feed on trees by probing and digging into bark with their beak to reach insect larvae and sap. They also use feeders, and some species feed on the ground using their strong feet to hop around.

Species include: red-bellied woodpecker, downy woodpecker, northern flicker, hairy woodpecker.

Hairy woodpecker

Northern cardinal

Sharp-shinned hawk

Flat feet

A great number of backyard birds have flat feet, with three short toes facing forward, and a hind claw. Some larger birds, such as thrushes and sparrows, prefer to feed on the ground or on flat surfaces, hopping around to collect food. These species are often heavier looking than the long-clawed birds, with more bulky body shapes, making them less mobile in trees. However, some flat-footed species, particularly songbirds, do perch in trees and use perches for feeding.

Species include: dark-eyed junco, white-throated sparrow, white-crowned sparrow, golden-crowned sparrow, song sparrow, American tree sparrow, purple finch, northern cardinal, American robin, wood thrush, Swainson's thrush, common grackle, gray catbird, mourning dove, blue jay.

Raptor feet

The feet of owls and hawks are adapted in different ways to those of most other birds as they use them to catch their food. Their sharp talons (claws) are perfectly formed for grabbing hold of prey, carrying it away, sometimes killing it, or holding it down while feeding. When you see a hawk or owl in the yard, it is typically looking for easy food.

Species include: eastern screech owl, sharp-shinned hawk, Cooper's hawk, American kestrel.

BEAK TYPE AND FEEDING

Noticing beak size and shape can tell you a lot about what a bird eats, and sometimes how it catches its food.

Backyard birds have a great variety of beak sizes and shapes that are specialized to enable the bird to obtain the food it needs. Some have evolved to extract insects from crevices, others to crack open tough seeds. Different types of bird feeders are accessible to birds with different beak types, so by knowing the beak type, you can provide a suitable feeder. There are six main beak types: short beaks, long beaks, finches, insect eaters, woodpeckers, and raptors.

Short beaks

Warblers and small ground-dwelling birds have short beaks to feed off readily available food. Their beaks are not designed to reach into depths for food but instead enable them to forage on flies, seeds, and berries. Sparrows have short, finch-like triangular beaks. These birds take well to food from tray or hanging feeders that is easy to eat and quick to pick up.
Species include: brown creeper, chickadees, scarlet tanager, red-eyed vireo, warblers, dark-eyed junco, sparrows.

Long beaks

Longer beaks are beneficial to birds that forage on the ground, as they can use their beaks to dig down in search of worms or into apples and other fruits. Thrushes use their long beaks to pull berries from thorny trees. Although mainly ground-feeding birds, those with long beaks will readily take apples, mealworms, and seed mixes put onto ground feeders.
Species include: American robin, wood thrush, Swainson's thrush, common grackle, gray catbird, mourning dove, blue jay.

White-throated sparrow

Swainson's thrush

Raptor beaks

Raptors have short, sharp, strong beaks. Some eat carrion, and all are predators. Birds of prey catch their food on the ground or in the air, using their feet, but they mostly go to a perch to eat it, holding larger items with the feet while tearing off pieces with the beak.

Species include: owls, hawks, and kestrels.

American kestrel

Insect-eater beaks

Beaks of insect eaters are small and pointed, with a wide mouth for catching insects mid-air. Bristles at the base of the beak help locate prey, or prevent insects entering the nasal passage or eyes. These birds visit yards with water and plants where insects gather.

Species include: chickadees, scarlet tanager, red-eyed vireo, warblers, swallows, purple martin, chimney swift.

American redstart

Woodpecker beaks

Large, thick, and sturdy, woodpeckers' beaks are ideal for pecking into bark or digging the ground in search of ants and other insects. Woodpeckers also have very long tongues, which curl around inside the back of the skull but can be extended to probe into bark cavities for beetle larvae or into anthills. The tongue is barbed and coated in sticky saliva to capture insects. They also use their beaks to break up and feed on nuts in feeders.

Species include: red-bellied woodpeckers, downy woodpeckers, hairy woodpeckers, northern flickers.

Northern flicker

Finch beaks

Finches have some of the most varied and remarkable beaks of all the perching songbirds. Their strong beaks range in size, some being ideal for crushing larger seeds, others being better for delicately picking soft seeds from flower heads. Some finches are especially fond of feeders with seeds or peanuts, and several are attracted by small, soft niger seed in special feeders.

Species include: purple finch, house finch, American goldfinch, evening grosbeak, pine siskin, common redpoll, red crossbill.

Evening grosbeak

WHAT TO FEED BIRDS

Food mixes vary from basic mixes, suitable for almost all birds, to highly specialized foods.

Providing the best food and feeders (*see pp.48–57*) for your birds is easier when you are familiar with the variety of food mixes available, and which birds they are suitable for. Some foods are best given at different times; for example giving more high-energy seeds benefits birds particularly during the breeding season and before migration.

Striped sunflower seeds

Hulled sunflower seeds

Sunflower seeds

Sunflower seeds provide exceptional nutritional value, especially in winter. Black oil seeds have very thin shells easily opened by seed-eating birds. Striped seeds have thicker shells and are harder for birds to open. Hulled sunflower seeds are ideal offerings for people living in apartments as there is no shell mess to clean up. Expect to attract jays, finches, chickadees, cardinals, juncos, siskins, titmice, and grosbeaks to trays, hoppers, tube, and window feeders containing sunflower seeds.

Black oil sunflower seeds

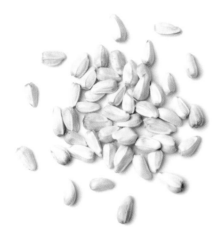

Safflower seeds

Safflower seeds are white in color and slightly smaller than black oil sunflower seeds. Like the latter, they are also high in protein, fat, and fiber, and are very nutritional for many backyard birds, including chickadees, cardinals, jays, finches, doves, and titmice. Another benefit of these seeds—house sparrows, starlings, and most squirrels don't like them!

Dried and fresh fruit

For birds that are not attracted to seed feeders, consider offering fresh or dried fruit. Orange halves, apple slices, cherries, grapes, and berries can be placed on platform or hanging feeders and are inviting to orioles, mockingbirds, robins, catbirds, towhees, waxwings, and other birds, as well as butterflies. Using an oven or food dehydrator, you can make dried fruit to offer birds in the winter to vary their diets.

Niger seeds

Niger seeds are tiny black seeds, the absolute favorite of many finches. You can buy specialized feeders for them as they are very fine, but you can also provide them through regular feeders with a tray underneath or on a solid tray feeder.

Peanuts

High in energy, unsalted peanuts are also high in entertainment as you watch birds feeding enthusiastically on them. Whole peanuts are mostly suitable for species with thicker bills such as woodpeckers, but also for birds such as nuthatches, which love to store their food. You can provide peanuts throughout the year, but it's good to put out more during the winter months and peak migration times to help birds build up an energy store. Choose peanuts prepared for birds without the shells on them, and feed whole peanuts in mesh feeders so that birds break them up with their beaks. Chopped peanuts are also available and can be mixed with other foods.

Mealworms

Dried mealworms are loved by insect-eating birds such as robins and bluebirds. They are a source of fat and protein and you can add them to mixes or feed them alone from a tray or ground feeder. In the breeding season, soak them in water overnight before putting them out to make them digestible for young birds.

Suet cakes

Suet cakes provide nutrients and fat in the same meal, with other food embedded in them such as insects or seeds. Some contain more fat than substance—you want to be able to see the substance, so look at the ingredients or even make your own (see pp.46–47).

Sugar water (Nectar)

Hummingbirds burn up lots of calories each day. They supplement their diet of tiny insects by zipping between nectar-rich flowers or visits to nectar feeders. You can prepare a solution of sugar water that mimics natural nectar by dissolving 1 part sugar with 4 parts water. Pour the mixture into a nectar feeder and hang it in a quiet shady area of the yard, preferably near a tree as hummers like to perch on branches between sips.

MAKE YOUR OWN BIRD FOOD MIX

Instead of buying food mixes, why not try creating your own using items from your fridge and pantry? Look at the type of consistency you want in your mix and adjust the elements as you wish. A classic mix consists of about 40 percent filler to give texture, 35 percent bulk, which is the main nutrition for the birds, and 25 percent fat for extra energy. To create a particularly high-energy mix, include more protein-based elements, such as peanuts or sunflower hearts. You can tailor the mix to suit the birds in your yard and alter it for the time of year, perhaps providing a mixture of fat and protein during the winter and at migration times for birds departing on their long route home. The easiest way to create your mix is to take two cups of filler, one cup of bulk, and half a cup of fat, put them into a bowl, and mix them together well. This mix can be served to your birds either in tube feeders or on tray feeders, depending on the mix you are creating.

- **Filler ingredients:** oats, crushed eggshells, cooked rice, cereal, fruit or vegetable seeds, crumbled pastry.
- **Bulk:** sunflower seeds (with or without hulls), chopped unsalted nuts, fruit or vegetable seeds, cereal, bread crumbs, cooked diced potato, raisins, other dried fruit, diced fruit peel.
- **Fat:** butter (unsalted), grated cheese, chunks of unsalted meat fat.

MAKE YOUR OWN SUET MIX

Suet balls or other shapes of suet mix are easy to make, and you can adapt the seed mix each time. Children can get involved in making these bird treats.

Seeds, nuts, and dried fruit pieces embedded in suet make a highly nutritious feast loved by many types of bird. You can make suet balls or blocks similar to those found for sale, but you can also adapt them into different shapes, or add suet to a mold such as a yogurt container, or fill half a coconut shell. Experiment with altering the seed mixes for different times of the year. A higher fat and protein mix might be a good choice to give an energy boost during the winter months or before migration, while softer and smaller seeds are more suitable for adult birds to feed to fledglings during the breeding season. Depending on their shape, your suet mix treats can be hung in trees or from feeding stations, or placed on a tray feeder.

1. Add your seed and suet
First, select the seed you want to use. You can buy ready-mixed seed or create your own mix. Add little chunks of vegetable suet.

2. Mix the ingredients
Use the warmth of your hands to soften the suet and mix it with the seed so they bind together to form a sticky and soft mixture.

3. Form into shapes

Start to mold the suet and seed mixture into the shape you want. Mold it carefully, making sure the seed and suet is evenly distributed. Smooth edges will hold together better in a feeder.

4. Put aside the shapes to set

Place the molded shapes in an open container in the fridge to firm up. Once they are set, put the shapes into your feeders.

MAKING ALTERNATIVE SHAPES

Cookie-cutter suet shapes

For smaller fingers, cookie cutters are the perfect way to shape your suet mix. Put the cutter onto a cookie sheet or solid surface and press the mixture into the shape, adding a hole for string. Leave it flat and allow it to firm up.

Suet blocks

Use empty yogurt containers to shape your suet mix. Add your mixture into the container, firming it down. Allow the mixture to firm up before removing the mold and placing the shapes in a feeder.

TYPES OF BIRD FEEDER

The many feeders available have been
designed with different birds and feed in mind.

When choosing a feeder, start by looking at which types of birds you would like to attract, then at what foods you need to provide for them (*see pp.42–45*). Group feeders into a feeding station in your yard (*see pp.58–59*). Some come with trays underneath to collect spilled feed—these are optional but useful to avoid mess and attracting pests (*see pp.148–149*).

Ground feeders

These are platforms on short legs close to the ground. Although you can just put the feed straight onto the ground, using a ground feeder ensures that you don't get a collection of seeds in one place, which can result in sprouting and the spread of mold. They're easy to clean and allow you to adapt your feeding. Ground feeders are more likely to attract larger birds; some smaller birds may be wary of visiting due to the higher risk of predators on the ground.

Suitable for: all types of birds, but particularly finches and those with flat feet and long beaks.

Tray feeders

Fully adaptable for any feed and any yard, tray feeders come in a variety of designs from sturdy platforms to dishes that hang from trees. They are available in different styles and materials including wood and metal. These trays are perfect for all types of food from seed mixes to suet cakes and are a great surface to mix up your feeding.

Suitable for: all types of birds, depending on the size of your tray.

Tube feeders

The most practical and adaptable bird feeders, these are made of metal and plastic. They are suitable for most mixes and come in a range of sizes, with some having two holes and others having of four or more. If you have flocks of birds or want to attract more species, then go for more holes. The perches range from metal bars to rounded stands; if you're opting for food that needs a bit of chewing, choose the rounded stand. A removable base makes it much easier to clean.

Suitable for: finches and birds with long claws, flat feet, and short beaks.

Mesh feeders

These feeders are suitable for larger items such as peanuts and suet pellets, but are not designed to be filled with seed mixes as the birds will struggle when retrieving seeds, or the seeds will fall out through the mesh. To access the food, birds need to be able to grasp hold of the bars and hang on to the feeder in order to feed; they also need enough bill strength to break up items such as peanuts.

Suitable for: birds with long claws such as chickadees, nuthatches, and woodpeckers.

Suet feeders

There is a wide variety of purpose-made suet-block feeders available for different shapes of block. Likewise for suet logs you can either put the logs in a suet-ball feeder or you can purchase a suet-log feeder and place the logs in the available holes.
Suitable for: woodpeckers and long-clawed birds such as chickadees and nuthatches.

Nectar feeders

Most nectar feeders are red, as hummingbirds are especially drawn to this color. Hummingbirds feed by probing a port with their long, slender bill while hovering or while resting on small perches. Because sugar water spoils quickly, it should be replaced every few days and feeders thoroughly cleaned once a week.
Suitable for: hummingbirds.

Window feeders

Not only for walls, these feeders can also be put onto fences and even house windows. Some come with suction cups to attach to windows, while others come with attachments for drilling into walls or fences. They are available in a variety of shapes for different-sized birds but the most common are the acrylic and the wooden house styles. As they are flat-bottomed or domelike, these can hold any sort of seed mixtures. **Suitable for:** some finches; long-clawed and short-beaked birds, such as juncos.

Hopper feeders

Hopper feeders are designed to hold enough seed to last several days and to keep seed dry and free of bird droppings. They are harder to clean than tray feeders. They can be hung from a branch or mounted on a post or pole. A squirrel baffle may be necessary to prevent them from climbing up to reach the feeder. **Suitable for:** finches, cardinals, jays, and chickadees.

OTHER WAYS TO FEED BIRDS

You can still provide food for birds that do not visit feeders. A log, tree trunk, or post with a little suet or cheese smeared into the cracks may draw woodpeckers, brown creepers, chickadees, tufted titmice, nuthatches, and yellow-rumped warblers (*right*). You could also drill holes into a log or post and put dried fruit or nuts into them.

MAKE YOUR OWN TUBE FEEDER

Easy to make, and an excellent use for old plastic bottles, these feeders make a useful addition for birds in your yard.

Make tube feeders out of clean, old plastic bottles in a variety of sizes, with either sticks or wooden spoons to serve as perches for your birds to feed from. These feeders are suitable for filling with classic seed mixes, high-energy mixes, and no-mess mixes, and are particularly good for birds that have short beaks (see p.40) and long claws (see p.38). You can place these feeders at feeding stations in your yard, hanging from a tree or fence, or on a balcony. Fill them up regularly and they will be irresistible to your backyard visitors.

1. Prepare your bottle

Choose your plastic bottle and clean it out thoroughly. Attach a piece of string, twine, or soft wire to the neck of the bottle ready for hanging later.

2. Make holes in the bottle

Use a scratch awl or other sharp tool to carefully poke two holes into your bottle opposite each other to fit the perches. Create another two holes, each up to $^3/_4$in (2 cm) in diameter, above the perch holes for birds to access the feed. Cover all the holes with tape for the time being.

3. Make perches for the birds

Choose either sticks or a wooden spoon and thread into the holes. Avoid any sharp edges.

Larger bottle feeders

It's not just small bottles you can transform into upcycled bird feeders. For a larger feeder you can use taller plastic drink bottles and repeat steps 2 and 3 to add one or two more feeding perches.

4. Fill your feeder and hang it in your yard

Pour a fine seed mix through the neck of the bottle—a funnel is useful to prevent spillage. Remove the tape covering the two feeding holes. Replace the bottle lid and hang up your new feeder.

Different bottle shapes

If you don't use plastic drink bottles, try large transparent plastic bottles from bathroom products or sauces. For instructions on how to make this feeder, see pp.54–55.

MAKE YOUR OWN
UPSIDE-DOWN FEEDER

*An upside-down feeder is an alternative design
that works with the seed trickling down
into a dish at the base.*

Different sorts of plastic bottles, including smaller ketchup and condiment bottles, can be made into a variation on the bottle feeder. Instead of adding sticks to the bottles to make them into perching feeders you can turn the bottle upside down and add a dish at the base so the seed will trickle down into it. The seed will only enter the dish to replace seed that has already been eaten. Be sure you clean out the bottle thoroughly beforehand with a gentle detergent so that residual smells do not taint the feed when birds visit.

1. Prepare your bottle
Make two holes for the string at the base of the bottle and thread through the string, twine, or soft wire.

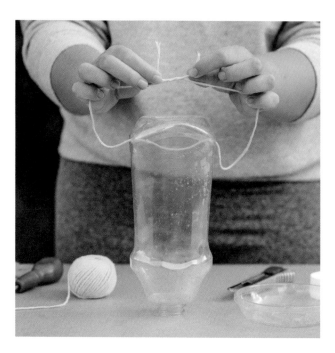

GLASS BOTTLE FEEDER

Although plastic bottles are light and easy to use, glass bottles, such as wine or oil bottles, are also suitable. You can create a wooden house to fit your bottle, with a dish or platform for birds to perch on to eat the seed. It is also possible to buy attachments to convert bottles into upside-down feeders.
Make sure to hang these feeders securely to avoid breakages.

2. Make holes for the seed

Pierce a few holes around the neck of the bottle; the seed will come out of these.

3. Add a dish at the base

Using string or cable ties, attach a small dish to the neck of the bottle for the seed to gather and for birds to perch on. Plastic dishes or saucers made to go under plant pots are ideal. Fill and hang up your new feeder in your yard (*right*).

MAKE YOUR OWN WINDOWED FEEDER

An alternative to add variety to your feeding station is to make a feeder with large openings, or windows, for birds to hop in and feed.

This design is slightly more complex to create as you will need bigger bottles and sharp tools to cut the windows neatly. Large plastic milk jugs are good for this particular design, but you can use other bottles, too. Bathroom or kitchen cleaning products often come in large, thick containers, which would be perfect for this design. As some of these bottles contain liquids that can be harmful to you and therefore the wildlife you are providing them for, you need to clean them out thoroughly before starting work on your upcycled feeder.

1. Prepare your bottle
Choose and clean your bottle, and loop and tie string, twine, or soft wire around the neck ready for your feeder to be hung up outside.

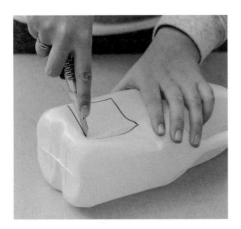

2. Make windows in the bottle

Using a sharp tool, such as a utility knife or pointed scissors, carefully cut two windows into opposite sides of your bottle. Make your windows large enough for the bird to perch in. If any edges are sharp, carefully sand them down.

JUICE CARTON FEEDER

During summer or dry spells, you can use juice cartons to create this design. They are not as strong as plastic jugs, especially when wet, and it is best to make slightly smaller windows to avoid putting too much strain on the carton when it contains bird feed.

3. Add seed

Use a scoop or cup to fill the base of your bottle with your chosen seed mix up to the level of the windows.

4. Put up your feeder

Hang your feeder in the yard. As this feeder has a shallow layer of seed in the base, check and refill it frequently.

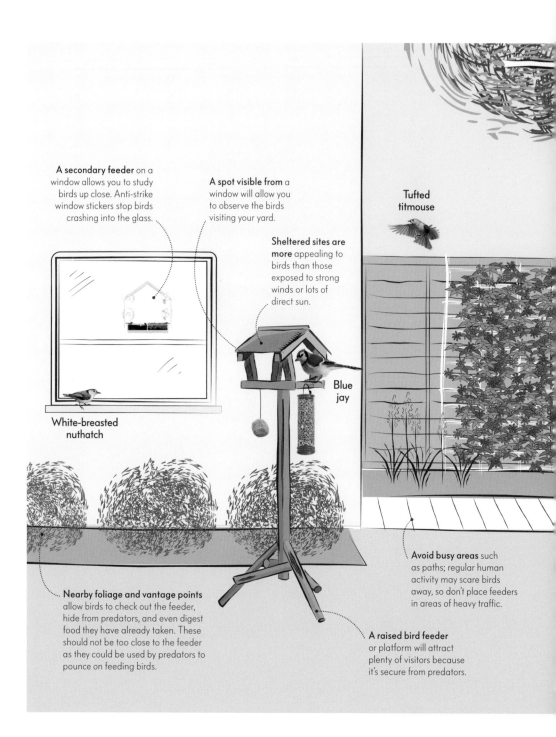

A secondary feeder on a window allows you to study birds up close. Anti-strike window stickers stop birds crashing into the glass.

A spot visible from a window will allow you to observe the birds visiting your yard.

Sheltered sites are more appealing to birds than those exposed to strong winds or lots of direct sun.

Tufted titmouse

White-breasted nuthatch

Blue jay

Nearby foliage and vantage points allow birds to check out the feeder, hide from predators, and even digest food they have already taken. These should not be too close to the feeder as they could be used by predators to pounce on feeding birds.

Avoid busy areas such as paths; regular human activity may scare birds away, so don't place feeders in areas of heavy traffic.

A raised bird feeder or platform will attract plenty of visitors because it's secure from predators.

CREATING A FEEDING STATION

Choosing your seed mixes and feeders is only the beginning. Next you need to choose the best place to put your feeders.

A feeding station is a collection of several types of feeders grouped together. Having a feeding station rather than a single feeder enables you to offer different foods in a variety of feeders so that a wide range of birds can feed, sometimes at the same time. Feeding stations can consist of a platform feeder with hooks underneath for additional feeders, a multi-armed metal feeding station, or a tree adorned with feeders. You can also create your own using scrap metal or wooden coat racks with multiple hooks for feeders.

Consider these factors when choosing where to position the station in your yard, balcony, or courtyard. Look at different areas from a bird's perspective: is there a lot of human or pet activity that might keep them away? Is the food easy to see? Birds need to feel safe: is there anywhere for them to perch and look for predators? Perches such as plants with foliage, or structures nearby, enable birds to move easily between the perch and the feeding station. Finally, put it in a spot that is easy for you to access to fill up and clean the feeders regularly.

House finch

Site a nest box far enough from the feeders so the nesting pair do not feel their territory is threatened by other birds.

Don't put feeders too near areas in which you grow vegetables, especially if you use pesticides.

This platform feeding station is slightly away from the main walkway, but visible from the house. The nearby tree and bushes offer cover and perches for birds.

POSITIONING SECONDARY FEEDERS

Shier birds may not receive enough food at the main feeding station; secondary feeders allow them and others to feed in a different part of the yard.

A lot of different birds can live and feed in the same area, although there is a natural hierarchy, and smaller birds may be deterred from feeding by larger or bolder ones. Secondary feeders are for birds that may not receive enough at the main feeding station (see pp.58–59), or they simply provide more or different sorts of food within the yard. If you switch your feeders from time to time, with specialists moving between your primary and secondary feeders, you can see which location and combination the birds prefer. Secondary feeders can be placed on fences, trees, windows, or at ground level.

Fences and sheds

If your main feeding station is in the middle of your yard, a secondary feeder on a fence or shed is a great option. This can simply be a tube feeder, wall feeder, or suet feeder. These suit smaller birds who find it easy to reach the feed.

Trees

If you have trees in your yard, consider using the tree for secondary feeders. Trees provide natural cover for birds to dart in and out, and are perfect for hanging a tray feeder or a selection of specialty feeders. You can also attach a feeder to the trunk.

Windows

For smaller yards and balconies, using what you have is vital. You can put a primary feeding station in your outdoor area and use your windows as a secondary feeding place. A number of feeders have adapters to fit them to windows, including suet-ball feeders and tray feeders. Birds sometimes fly toward reflections such as trees in the glass, then collide with the window, stunning or killing themselves. To prevent this, place window stickers near your feeder to show birds there is a hard surface there to be avoided.

Ground feeders

No matter the space you have, you can always use ground feeders to attract larger bird species away from your primary feeding stations. Providing some extra food on your ground feeder draws in the larger birds, enabling the smaller birds to feed at your primary feeders.

Position a secondary feeder wherever you have space, and experiment with different locations or add more feeders. Clockwise from top: Baltimore oriole at feeder with an orange; eastern bluebirds at a mealworm feeder; tray feeder; finches on a mesh tube feeder.

COMBINING FEEDERS, FOOD, AND BIRDS

Feeder type	Food type	Beak type	Foot type	Birds that may visit
Tube feeder	• Classic mix • High-energy mix • No-mess mix	• Short beaks • Finches	• Long claws • Flat feet	Carolina chickadee, house finch, white-breasted nuthatch, pine siskin, common redpoll, common grackle
Mesh feeder	• Peanuts	• Woodpeckers	• Long claws • Woodpeckers	Red-bellied woodpecker, hairy woodpecker, downy woodpecker, white-breasted nuthatch, black-capped chickadee
Tray feeder	• Classic mix • High-energy mix • Ground mix • Peanuts	• Long beaks • Short beaks • Finches	• Long claws • Flat feet	Baltimore oriole, scarlet tanager, tufted titmouse, blue jay, Steller's jay, brown-headed cowbird, chipping sparrow, purple finch, northern cardinal, red-breasted nuthatch, Carolina chickadee
Ground feeder	• No-mess mix • Ground mix • Peanuts	• Long beaks • Short beaks • Finches	• Long claws • Flat feet	American crow, mourning dove, blue jay, Steller's jay, common grackle, northern cardinal, hermit thrush, northern mockingbird, red-winged blackbird, white-throated sparrow, American robin

Feeder type	Food type	Beak type	Foot type	Birds that may visit
Wall feeder	• Classic mix • High-energy mix • Peanuts	• Short beaks • Finches	• Long claws	Black-capped chickadee, tufted titmouse, Carolina wren, chipping sparrow, common redpoll, house finch, red-breasted nuthatch, pine siskin, yellow-rumped warbler
Suet-ball feeder	• Suet balls • Suet logs	• Short beaks • Woodpeckers	• Long claws • Woodpeckers	Downy woodpecker, hairy woodpecker, red-bellied woodpecker, white-breasted nuthatch
Suet feeder	• Suet block • Suet logs	• Short beaks • Woodpeckers	• Long claws • Woodpeckers	Downy woodpecker, hairy woodpecker, red-bellied woodpecker, white-breasted nuthatch
Niger feeder	• Niger seed	• Finches	• Long claws	American goldfinch, common redpoll, black-capped chickadee, pine siskin, purple finch

HOW TO MAINTAIN YOUR FEEDERS

Cleaning your bird feeders regularly is vital for keeping birds healthy by helping prevent the spread of disease and bacteria.

Birds share feeders, and regular cleaning, two to three times per month, is essential to prevent the buildup of harmful bacteria on surfaces. There are a number of widespread diseases that affect backyard birds (*see pp.152–153*), and keeping feeders clean is a key part in controlling these.

Being adaptable

A regular cleaning session is an opportunity to assess how much food you put out. Much as your backyard visitors may love the food you provide, sometimes not all of the seeds and food are eaten, resulting in mold or sprouting seeds within the feeders, as well as wasted food.

Look at the amount of each food that your birds are eating. If a particular type is regularly left over you can reduce the quantity of that food next time you refill the feeders. You can also move your feeders around to a different part of the yard, which prevents droppings (and sprouted seeds) building up in one area, and may deter rodents which visit an area for leftover food.

Summer feeder care

Birds are less likely to visit feeders in the summer when natural food sources are abundant, so consider putting out less food for a few months. Even with this reduction in food, you should give your feeders an extra clean per month during warm spells, as bacteria are more likely to develop and food will go moldy more quickly.

Clean your feeders both inside and out and leave them to dry thoroughly to prevent disease.

HOW TO CLEAN YOUR FEEDERS

Clean several feeders at once outside using rubber gloves and cleaning equipment you keep especially for this purpose. Follow the tips below, then leave your feeders to dry out thoroughly—if you put food into a damp feeder it will start to go moldy. Consider buying or making some back-up feeders that you can put out while your other feeders are being washed and dried.

Empty out old food

Start by emptying and discarding old food. Don't use it to refill the feeder or put it on the compost heap—both may spread disease.

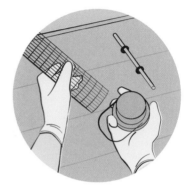

Take apart your feeder

It's really worth taking apart your feeder to give it a thorough wash. Remove the base and take out the perches. Some need unscrewing, so make sure to keep all the parts safe to reassemble later.

Soak well

If you're finding it hard to remove old food, soak the feeders for a while in warm water before you start scrubbing them.

Scrub every surface and corner

Use a nail brush or old toothbrush to give your feeder a good scrub in warm water with dish detergent or mild disinfectant. Scrub around the base and over the perches to dislodge old seeds.

NESTING

NESTING

Birds make nests in a safe place so they can lay eggs and raise their young. You can encourage more birds to nest in your yard by providing well-situated birdhouses. If birds breed and nest in your yard, you will be rewarded by seeing courtship behavior, territorial disputes, and young birds being fed.

Eastern bluebirds readily take to birdhouses and can raise two to three broods of chicks per year.

WHY HAVE A BIRDHOUSE?

A birdhouse makes a great addition to a wildlife-friendly yard, by providing birds with a safe space to raise the next generation.

One reason why bird numbers are in decline is a lack of nesting spaces. All too often trees and vegetation on land that developers will use to build houses are cut down and removed. Trees and shrubs subsequently planted in yards are usually small and take some years to grow and mature. You can counter this habitat loss, no matter the size of your outdoor space. A birdhouse or nest box gives birds a ready-made home that provides the basic conditions of their natural nesting site: some are small and cozy like the holes in trees where chickadees nest, while others are long and deep to create more space and darkness for birds such as owls, or cup-shaped to replicate nests of swallows. In some ways, birdhouses can even be a better option for birds than natural sites, since a well-made house can provide safe shelter from predators, and is more likely to still be there when the birds return the following year.

What you will see

You can get great enjoyment from watching birds visit their birdhouse, and waiting for the young fledglings to emerge into the world. Birds that nest in your yard will forage constantly for caterpillars and aphids—pests that might otherwise harm your plants—to feed their young. Not all birds use birdhouses; some are open nesters and prefer to nest naturally. But many will readily use a house, making nests inside in the breeding season with material they find nearby. Owls and wrens are among those that also use houses for evening roosting, often returning to the same house each year.

Choosing a birdhouse

There is a huge selection of boxes available to buy, with designs to suit your style, as well as ones that you can fit a camera inside. You can also make one yourself (see pp.80–81). The design and location of your box and the size of the hole or opening (see pp.72–73) will determine which birds will nest in it, so look at which birds visit your yard or nearby and choose a birdhouse suitable for them.

House wrens feel safe in a house with a very small entrance hole so that predators cannot put their heads inside.

STANDARD BIRDHOUSES

*Encourage certain birds to nest in your
space by choosing the right birdhouse.*

Birdhouses create the conditions that a bird seeks in nature. These pages focus on a standard round-hole house design; the size of the hole will determine which types of birds can enter (*see opposite*). Other birdhouse designs are more specialized (*see pp.76–77*), with a particular size and shape to fit the natural nesting behavior of the bird.

Most garden centers and local hardware stores sell a range of birdhouses, although stores at specialty nature reserves and websites offer a much more comprehensive choice. Before buying, you need to know what features to look for in order to choose a resilient, long-lasting, easy-to-clean house. It's also quite easy, and often cheaper, to make your own (*see pp.80–81*).

Sloping roof
Slope allows rain water to run off, minimizing dampness inside.

Metal guard around entrance
Protects the entrance hole, maintaining the size so larger birds don't damage the house.

Wooden sides
Natural material blends in well in the yard and is breathable.

Hole height
An entrance hole needs to be at least 5 in (125 mm) above the floor of the house; otherwise, small hatchlings may risk falling or scrambling out too early.

Materials

Most standard birdhouses are made of wood. The wood should be breathable, solid, and not treated with any chemicals. An increasingly popular alternative is a blend of wood fiber and concrete, molded into shape. It is heavier than wood but lasts longer and does not rot. Avoid houses with metal sides and roofs, as they absorb too much heat.

Roof

The ideal roof should allow water to run off it, keeping the house dry inside. It can be set at an angle with a central apex, or sloped forward or backward, or even be curved. An overhanging roof also prevents water from getting into the entrance. A few designs come with a removable or hinged roof, which makes for easier cleaning.

Drainage and ventilation

Some houses have small gaps in the floor to allow air to circulate and for water and droppings to drain away. Since wood is breathable, this also allows air to pass in and out of the house.

Entrance holes

Some houses come with metal guards around the holes to stop woodpeckers from drumming into the holes to make them bigger. If you want to adapt your house for smaller birds, you can buy metal plates with different-sized holes; these can also be useful to repair damaged holes.

ENTRANCE HOLE SIZES

Here you can see two of the more common birdhouse entrance hole sizes. Before buying a house, make sure that the hole will be the correct size for the birds you are hoping to attract.

1–1¼ in (26–30 mm) hole

Small birds feel secure in houses with a hole of this size, knowing that larger species will struggle to enter to disturb their nest and young.
Suitable for: White-breasted nuthatch, black-capped chickadee, house wren.
Ideal position: 5–6½ ft (1.5–2 m) above the ground.

1¼–1½ in (28–38 mm) hole

Ideal for a variety of slightly larger birds, including tufted titmice, which may otherwise attempt to use a smaller-holed box. By providing a variety of hole sizes, you'll reduce competition for space between different species.
Suitable for: Flycatcher, tufted titmouse, tree swallow.
Ideal position: 5–6½ ft (1.5–2 m) above the ground.

OTHER COMMON BIRDHOUSES

Swallows, kestrels, and even owls can be persuaded to nest if the right house is provided.

In addition to standard round-holed houses (*see pp.72–73*), cup-shaped and open nesting shelters are designed to suit the particular needs of a range of birds, including migratory species that live their lives mainly in the air, catching their insect food on the wing, and owls and kestrels whose traditional nesting places have been reduced in number or lost.

Barn swallow nesting cups

Breeding barn swallows naturally make nests from mud and saliva adjacent to beams in sheds and barns, but often their nests crumble when the young fledge, or they fall down over the winter. Providing them with a ceramic nesting cup ensures their nest remains intact year after year and will be ready and waiting for them once they return from their migrations. The cups are sold attached to a piece of wood to allow it to be easily drilled into place, with a droppings board 36 in (1 m) below if necessary.
Ideal position: inside an outbuilding or garage (provided the birds can gain access through an open door).

Cliff swallow nesting cups

Unlike barn swallows' open-topped nest design, cliff swallows prefer to make a gourd-like mud nest tightly sealed usually under the peak of the roof line or against sides of bridges and culverts, with a small front entrance for access. Cliff swallow nesting cups mimic this design. Droppings often form a pile on the ground under their nests; if you want to avoid this mess, install a waste droppings board 24 in (60 cm) below the nest.
Ideal position: under the eaves of houses or near peak of roof line.

Open-nesting shelter

This shelf-style nest box is great for birds that typically like to nest in dense undergrowth for protection, as well as those that favor larger or circular nests. The open front and deep base allow the nesting bird to sit securely within the box while still being able to easily observe its surroundings through the wide window, just as they otherwise would if nesting within the undergrowth.

Suitable for: American robin, mourning dove, eastern phoebe.

Ideal position: Under the eaves or secured to a tree. Mount at least 6 ft (1.8 m) above ground to avoid predators.

Raptor box

Birds of prey, like screech owls and kestrels, may struggle to find suitable nesting locations. They often prefer to nest in trees near open land, so if your yard offers these conditions you can put up a raptor box to help them. Screech owls and kestrels can use the same size nest box. They can be secured to a tree, outbuilding, or mounted on a pole. The entry hole should face south or east.

Suitable for: screech owl, kestrel.

Ideal position: 10–30 ft (3–9 m) from the ground; under the cover of trees for owls; with open access on the fringes of a field for kestrels.

SPECIALITY BIRDHOUSES

Species including woodpeckers and chimney swifts can be attracted with specialized houses.

Although we may assume that birds will take to a house of a certain size and hole, some species have a particular way of nesting, which requires a different style or placement of house to meet their natural needs. This might involve providing purple martins with a conducive nesting environment or offering chimney swifts standalone chimney towers to swoop into.

Purple martin house

Purple martins are very social birds, nearly completely dependent on human-made nesting shelters, and they nest in colonies. They prefer either a single structure "apartment-like" house or individual houses arranged in a cluster. A commonly used individual house is a hollow natural or plastic gourd.

Ideal position: in open spaces 40–60ft (12–18m) away from any tall trees and 12–20ft (3.7–6m) above the ground, to avoid predators.

Eastern bluebird house

Bluebird houses look like standard round-hole boxes but are deeper, with 1½in (38mm) entrance holes to keep starlings out. They should be mounted 5–7ft (1.5–2.2m) off the ground in open areas with scattered trees and ready access to an insect supply.

Ideal position: on metal or wooden posts in an open area away from buildings.

Woodpecker box

Very similar to a standard birdhouse in its outward design, a woodpecker box is deep enough for the woodpecker to incubate its eggs and for the chicks to grow as they would in their natural nesting hole in a tree. It often has a piece of bark over the entrance hole, enabling the birds to excavate the hole (although this is not essential). Some also come with ladder grooves in the inside front of the box for the young fledglings to come out when they are ready. The size of the box and its hole will determine the type of woodpecker it will attract.
Ideal position: on a tree trunk, 10–16ft (3–5m) off the ground.

Brown creeper box

Brown creepers typically nest in crevices behind loose tree bark using their long claws to grip on to the bark and to move into their nests. With fewer mature, thick barked trees in neighborhood yards and parks to nest in, a brown creeper box is a great alternative. These boxes come in wood or a woven design with an opening on the side (see image).
Ideal position: on a tree trunk, so the brown creeper can climb relatively unobtrusively from the trunk into the box.

Chimney swift tower

The past few decades has seen a concerning decline in chimney swift populations as their principal roosting and nesting sites, old chimneys, have deteriorated, been capped, or removed. New chimney designs are not suited to swifts' needs. In an effort to counter this loss of habitat, some communities, conservation organizations, and individual homeowners have built chimney swift towers. These are 12ft (4m)-tall, freestanding structures designed for these nesting and roosting birds.
Ideal position: in open backyards or parks where there is clear, unobstructed access to the interior of the tower.

NESTING POCKETS

Designed for birds with particular nesting and roosting needs, pouches and pockets offer an alternative to classic birdhouses.

Nesting pockets (sometimes known as pouches) are designed to recreate the nest shapes preferred by particular types of birds, such as those that prefer to create rounded nests, which can be difficult to form within an angular wooden house. They are made from a blended mixture of materials to mimic a more natural structure, and can be placed in a sheltered spot within a shrub, bush, or, for some designs, on buildings.

Depending on its size, a pocket or pouch may also provide birds with a safe place to roost communally during the winter months. Winter wrens, chickadees, and nuthatches, for example, naturally huddle together for additional warmth. You can find these as woven baskets or shaped wooden boxes, usually from specialty birdhouse suppliers. The woven pockets don't last long, but do offer a safe, natural place for roosting.

Teardrop
Teardrop-shaped designs are perfect for species looking to roost or nest in deeper pockets, such as chickadees or wrens. Place just inside the foliage of a shrub or tree with string to hold it in place, or nestled as firmly as possible among the foliage.

Side pocket

These side pockets are for species that like an easy exit, including nuthatches and wrens. Settle the pocket into a shrub or place it in the crook of a tree.

Canopy

Canopy pockets are designed to be occupied by open-nesting species, like thrushes and doves. The pockets have open sides to mimic an open nesting site, but provide the shelter of a roof and more stability on the sides. Position the pocket among the foliage of a shrub or tie it to branches.

MAKE YOUR OWN BIRDHOUSE

With a little preparation, it's inexpensive and straightforward to make a home for nesting and roosting birds in your yard.

This project keeps things simple, as you only need one piece of wood and a few tools. The design and proportions can be adapted depending on the tools and materials you have on hand; for instance, if you don't have a hole saw, you could instead halve the height of the front piece and use it to create an open-fronted house. If you aren't comfortable using power tools, ask a friend to help you hold the pieces steady as you screw them together.

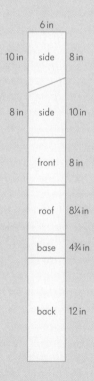

YOU WILL NEED

- Tape measure
- Pencil
- Untreated wooden board from a sustainable source (for our birdhouse we used a 50 in x 6 in plank)
- Drill
- Screwdriver and screws
- Hammer and nails
- Hole saw
- Metal or recycled rubber hinge

1. Mark the house pieces

Using a tape measure and pencil, mark on your piece of wood all the sections of the birdhouse you will need, as shown above.

2. Cut out the pieces

Carefully cut out each of the pieces, then drill holes for screws into the back and side pieces as shown in the photo above.

3. Attach sides, base, and back

Attach the two sides to the back piece by screwing up into the sides, then screw the base to the side pieces, leaving a gap between the base and back for drainage and air circulation.

4. Make an entrance hole

Mark out the hole at least 5 in from the base, making sure that it is the right size (*see p.72*). Use a hole saw tool to cut out the hole. Attach the front piece to the two side pieces.

5. Add the roof

Attach your roof with a hinge, either a metal one or some rubber from a bicycle inner tube or old rain boots. Cut off a rectangle of rubber and nail it to the roof and back to form a flexible, water-resistant hinge.

6. Put up your birdhouse

Finally, hang up the house in your desired location, in a sheltered spot away from direct sun and wind.

UPCYCLING BIRDHOUSES

Birds are naturally curious and ingenious in their nesting habits and sometimes choose unusual places to nest.

You can take advantage of birds' innate curiosity by providing quirky nesting places adapted from everyday objects. Make these upcycled birdhouses over the winter and position them ready for the start of the nesting season so birds have plenty of time to explore and find them. There is no one way to make an upcycled birdhouse, but these are some possibilities.

Old boots

Hiking boots, rain boots, work boots—just about any kind of worn-out boot can be adapted into a nesting spot for birds. For a hiking boot, screw the toe onto a piece of wood, with sides and a roof if desired (*see right*). Having the boot toe-down minimizes water entering the nest, but also creates a dark pocket which imitates a birdhouse. For a longer boot, attach the boot upright, cover the opening so rain doesn't get in, and make an entrance hole. The more waterproof the boots are, the more suitable they are to be hung up in the open on fences or in outbuildings such as sheds or barns. **Suitable for:** wren, nuthatch, chickadee.

Hanging baskets

Perfect substitute sites for birds that make fairly open nests, hanging baskets come in a variety of sizes that will suit different birds. You can put natural nesting material within the basket itself such as moss, twigs, feathers, and animal fur to make it more inviting to nest in (see pp.90–91). Hang your basket from a small evergreen tree such as bay laurel, or, if the basket is quite large, on the branch of an oak, alder, or conifer.
Suitable for: mourning dove, house finch.

Teapots

A variety of kitchen items can be used to offer birds a home in your yard; a colander, for instance, can be hung up in a manner similar to a hanging basket (see above). An old teapot can make a particularly curious addition to your birdhouse collection. Hang it up from the handle, and the spout underneath will act as drainage for any nesting birds. Make sure that the teapot is hung up securely; it can be nestled into a hedge or tree, then secured with string so that it does not become dislodged.
Suitable for: robin, mourning dove, Eastern phoebe, house finch.

Plastic bottle crates

Some birds, such as thrushes and other open nesters, prefer a nesting "shelf," while others prefer to nest in colonies. Plastic bottle crates are perfect for both of these. They can be placed on their sides on ledges or under eaves in outbuildings, or behind potted shrubs in smaller spaces and on balconies. Adding some straw, moss, or twigs to the bottom as a base will entice the birds and make the crate appealing as a nesting site. Alternatively, if you have a milk bottle crate, you can place a front on each of the squares and add some separators to make it into a communal birdhouse.
Suitable for: robin, mourning dove, Eastern phoebe, house finch.

PUTTING UP BIRDHOUSES

Birdhouse placement, more often than not, depends on what species you are hoping to attract.

Ideally, place a birdhouse facing north to east. This allows the house to escape the harshest weather such as direct sunlight and driving rain. If the house is in shade or a sheltered location, then it can face in any direction. Tilt your house slightly forward so the rain can run off the roof. Different houses need to be different heights off the ground (*see under specific houses, pp.76–77*), but a general rule is to allow at least 5–6½ft (1.5–2m) from the ground, to deter predators. Ensure there are no flat surfaces around the house itself, such as shelves, walls, or platforms, which could make a good ledge for a predator, such as a cat, to pounce from.

Wherever you intend to position your birdhouse (*see right*), secure it in place using galvanized screws about 3in (85mm) long, as they will not rust. Make sure the birdhouse is secure each winter before the start of the breeding season.

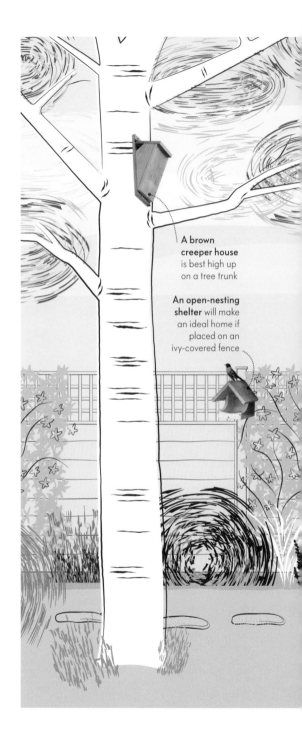

A brown creeper house is best high up on a tree trunk

An open-nesting shelter will make an ideal home if placed on an ivy-covered fence

Swallow nesting cups should be placed beneath the eaves of a building

A small-holed house should be positioned at least 5ft (1.5m) above the ground

WHERE TO PLACE YOUR BIRDHOUSES

Tree

The majority of houses, especially larger ones (*see p.75*), are suitable for placing in trees. Ensure there is an open space around the entrance; this will help deter predators, while also giving the parents a good flight path into the house.

Fence

Small birdhouses can be screwed directly into the fence itself using 3in (85mm) galvanized screws. Avoid attaching a support as it may become unstable and come loose over time. You can use a fence that is partly covered with vines (*see pp.108–109*), but avoid areas with too much vegetation where predators can hide. Plants near the fence can provide a good spot for parents to perch en route to and from the house.

Brick or cement wall

Drill a hole into the wall, insert an anchor, and use a galvanized 3in (85mm) screw to attach the birdhouse.

Balcony

If attaching a birdhouse to a balcony, position it as high up as possible so that it is less likely to be disturbed. Ensure it is within the balcony area so there is no risk of it falling onto the ground below.

HOW BIRDS DEVELOP

Discover what's going on inside your birdhouses, so you know what to look for when you monitor them.

Before you monitor your houses (see pp.88–89), it helps to understand a typical bird's breeding and nesting behavior. You'll find that the female lays and incubates the eggs, while the male supplies food and aids in gathering nesting material. Most species lay intermittently, meaning they will lay an egg every other day, covering them whenever they leave the nest. They will not incubate until all eggs have been laid, so they will ideally hatch within a few days of one another. At this stage, the adult birds take turns feeding their young until they are ready to leave the nest. For specific developmental information, check the Bird Profiles (see pp.158–185).

WHAT'S HAPPENING IN THE NEST?

1. Adult gathering material
Typically, the adult bird picks materials in the nearby area and brings them back to the nest, creating a layer around 1in (2.5 cm) deep.

2. Nesting
The material is woven to create a soft bowl shape. This allows the female to lay flat, and will later retain heat around the eggs to incubate them.

3. Eggs covered
If the adult leaves the nest during laying, she may cover her eggs with more material in order to hide and protect them from predators.

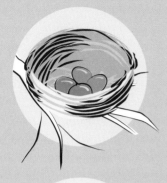

4. Eggs uncovered
This is the later part of the egg-laying process, indicating that the incubation stage is about to start.

5. Adult on nest
The adult bird incubates the eggs. Depending on the species, this stage may last for a week or more before the eggs hatch.

6. Blind young
The young will look like helpless naked birds with their eyes shut as their feathers begin to form (*see box, right*).

7. Ready to fly
Once the feathers fully fledge (*see right*), the young birds are able to leave the nest and fly short distances as they learn how to find food.

HOW FEATHERS GROW
As feathers grow, they are protected by a sheath, from which they emerge over time in a series of stages:
- **Pin:** at this stage, the wing and tail feathers are prickly and new, mainly consisting of the shaft.
- **Short:** this describes feathers that are less than one-third emerged from this sheath.
- **Medium:** the feathers are now between one- and two-thirds emerged from the sheath.
- **Large:** this describes feathers that are more than two-thirds developed from the sheath.
- **Fledged:** the feathers are now fully grown, with no sheath remaining.

Pin   Short   Medium   Large

MONITORING BIRDHOUSES

Watching your nest from a distance and visiting it to record what you see is rewarding and gives an insight into the breeding cycle.

It's exciting to watch your birdhouses being inspected by various birds, then nesting material being brought in, followed by beaks full of food, and the eventual exit of the fledging young. Keeping a careful eye on your birdhouses will enable you to trace what stage the birds are at in their growth and development (*see pp.86–87*).

Monitoring can be simply observing carefully from a distance. Or you can visit the nest on a few occasions. There are a number of guidelines to follow when going to inspect and monitor your birdhouses, and it is vital not to disturb the young birds and their parents. When monitoring your birdhouse, spend a minimal amount of time in close proximity to the house and do not visit more than once a week. Avoid disturbing nearby vegetation and don't dislodge the house.

The best way is to approach the house and lift the lid slowly and carefully, making sure young nestlings cannot jump out. Peer inside (not too closely), take a mental note of what you see, then shut the lid and leave the area of the house in the opposite direction from your approach before stopping to record what you see. If you do not have a house with a lid that can be lifted, you can use an endoscope or a dental mirror and feed it through the entrance hole to peer inside.

By observing what goes on inside your birdhouses, you'll encounter sights like these newly hatched young birds, still blind and without any sign of feather development.

You can adapt a regular birdhouse to accommodate a camera setup, or buy a prebuilt camera box like this, which has a space in the roof designed to house the camera securely.

Using a camera

A less intrusive way to see inside is to attach a specially-made camera. These can fit within any size house, enabling you to watch nesting birds as they rear their young or roost within your houses. You can buy a camera to fit into an existing house, or a house pre-fitted with a camera (see above). Some offer features such as a wide-angle lens so you can see as much as possible of what is going on in the nest, night-vision technology to allow the camera to see in dark houses, and high-quality images that can be streamed directly to your phone or computer.

In addition to deciding whether you want to buy a birdhouse already fitted with a camera, or whether to attach one into a regular birdhouse yourself, consider which type of power setup would suit your needs best (see right). All are available to purchase from wildlife stores and websites, and are sold as kits that are easy to set up.

POWER SETUPS

There are two main types of power setup: electric and battery powered. Both have their advantages, depending on your yard and the time you have available.

Electric power setup

This camera is fitted within the house with the electrical cable coming out of a small hole at the side of the house. An electric power source is required to keep the camera running, as well as a connection (via a cable or Wi-Fi) to a television or monitor to watch your box.

Battery power setup

This setup features a camera inside the house, with a battery attachment either inside or outside. Like electric power setups, these use either a cable or Wi-Fi to connect to your television or monitor. It is slightly more time-consuming as you will need to check battery life and change batteries as needed.

PUTTING OUT NESTING MATERIAL FOR BIRDS

With the loss of many natural places for birds to search for nesting material, you can lend a hand by providing what they need.

In addition to the natural materials that birds collect to add structure to their nests, including moss and twigs, there's a vast amount of material we use in our everyday lives that nesting birds can use (*see opposite*). You can put out a large quantity of any of these items as they won't cause harm by getting caught around birds' feet or around the young birds. Avoid unsafe materials, including plastic (which may get tangled around birds' feet) or any foliage that has been treated with pesticides (*see opposite*).

Choose a spot to put out the materials, perhaps on trees or on a feeding tray so the birds know where to find them. You can create your own nesting stocking or use a suet block feeder (*see opposite*), or even pack your chosen materials into an old whisk and hang it up.

Filling a suet block feeder with nesting material

Fill your block feeder with one material or a mixture of materials. If you wish, you could attach several blocks together with cable ties to form a square to provide more material and enable more birds to visit at a time.

Making a nesting material stocking

Fill the toe end of an old, long cotton or wool sock or pair of tights with nesting material. Tie a knot, fill the next section with another material, tie another knot, and so on, until you run out of room. In each bundle, cut a slit to enable the birds to reach the material. Hang up the stocking.

WHAT TO PUT OUT:

- Feathers
- Small yarn trimmings
- Moss
- Small pieces of natural cloth
- Shredded paper
- Hay
- Animal fur

WHAT NOT TO PUT OUT:

- String
- Mesh material
- Plastic (including cellophane)
- Foil
- Human hair
- Foliage that has been treated with any pesticides or chemicals

CLEANING YOUR BIRDHOUSE

Clearing out your birdhouse at the end of the season is vital to prevent the buildup of pests and to make the house ready for the following spring.

The best time to clean out a birdhouse is after the breeding season, when fledglings have left the nest for good. It should be recognized that native migratory and nonmigratory birds are protected by law, and you cannot disturb them, their nests, eggs, or habitats during the breeding season. Before you get ready to clean out your birdhouse, observe it over a number of weeks to make sure that there is no sign of any activity, as some birds may choose to roost in the house or small mammals may shelter inside it during the winter months.

Clearing and cleaning houses

Always wear gloves when cleaning and handling birdhouses, to minimize the risk of flea bites. Remove all material from the inside of your house and lay it to one side. Clean your birdhouse with hot water and use a strong scrubbing brush to ensure no parasites or bacteria are living within the crevices of the birdhouse. Leave it to dry.

While the house is drying, sort through the nesting material that you have taken out. Throw away or compost anything that is decaying, such as remains, unhatched eggs, and nesting

Remove all loose material from inside the birdhouse, and scrape away any material stuck to the sides.

Always wear gloves when handling and cleaning out used birdhouses.

materials covered with droppings. These can all harbor parasites and fleas, which will infest young birds the following year if not removed.

Once the birdhouse has fully dried, fill it with some fresh wood shavings which will provide extra comfort for any roosting birds during the winter.

PLANTING

PLANTING

If chosen well, plants can provide both shelter and a source of food for birds, helping them thrive. By adding more bird-friendly plants to your yard, you are adding life and interest in the form of foliage, flowers, nesting materials, and food, so birds can find what they need all year.

American robins are among many species that rely on a succession of fruits and berries for their diet in fall and winter.

GARDENING FOR BIRDS

Birds are part of a yard's ecosystem. If all parts of the system are working well, both the yard and its wildlife will flourish.

How you choose to garden can bring enormous benefits to birds and other wildlife. Although birds will visit any green space, they are more likely to visit one that meets their needs; this chapter will explore those needs, along with some specific plants that offer particular benefits to birds. Gardening for wildlife can mean anything from devoting an area to shrubs to simply planting a pot of native wildflowers on a patio. Whatever you decide to do to encourage more wild visitors, work toward a more natural, healthy balance in the space, starting from the ground up (*see below*).

THE IMPORTANCE OF SOIL HEALTH

Healthy soil is not only key for healthy plants but for the whole ecosystem. It has a huge effect on soil-dwelling invertebrates, including worms, grubs, and the larvae of many moth and beetle species—all creatures that birds feed on. To help your soil thrive, add organic matter such as compost or well-rotted manure to it. Avoid using slug pellets, pesticides, or insecticides, as these do not discriminate between killing undesirable insects and beneficial ones, such as pollinators. Your aim should be to keep your plants healthy and give wildlife a space in your yard; both can be achieved.

Flowers for birds and insects
Pollen- and nectar-rich plants in borders or containers provide food for insects, which the birds in turn can feast upon. Some butterflies rest on the heads of dill while blooms of bee balm beckon both butterflies and hummingbirds.

Black swallowtail butterfly

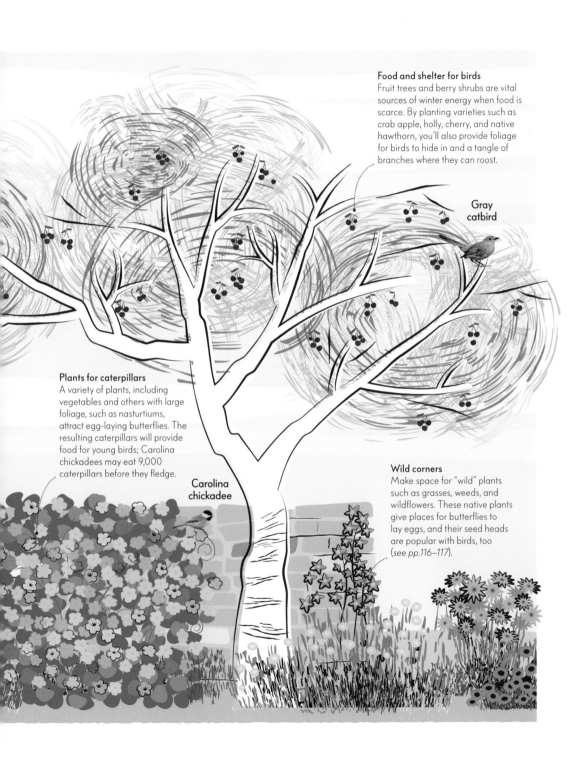

Food and shelter for birds
Fruit trees and berry shrubs are vital sources of winter energy when food is scarce. By planting varieties such as crab apple, holly, cherry, and native hawthorn, you'll also provide foliage for birds to hide in and a tangle of branches where they can roost.

Gray catbird

Plants for caterpillars
A variety of plants, including vegetables and others with large foliage, such as nasturtiums, attract egg-laying butterflies. The resulting caterpillars will provide food for young birds; Carolina chickadees may eat 9,000 caterpillars before they fledge.

Carolina chickadee

Wild corners
Make space for "wild" plants such as grasses, weeds, and wildflowers. These native plants give places for butterflies to lay eggs, and their seed heads are popular with birds, too (see pp.116–117).

WHAT PLANTS PROVIDE

Plants attract and support birdlife throughout the year, providing nesting materials, shelter, and food.

The plants in your yard should ideally provide five key elements for birds (*see below*). The more you have, the greater the variety of bird species you are likely to attract. It's not about how much space you have, but how many different nesting, feeding, and shelter options your yard offers.

How you garden will also help draw birds to your space. Leaving seed heads on after the flowers have finished blooming, locating plants to create safe spaces for nesting and sheltering without fear of predators, choosing flowers that will attract maximum insect activity (and therefore provide plenty of food for birdlife)—these are a few of the many strategies to use in your space.

Privet *(Ligustrum)*, with its dense foliage, offers a good hiding spot for birds.

Hornbeam *(Carpinus)* is a favorite for birds, providing nesting materials, shelter, and nutlets.

Small twigs

Foliage

FIVE KEY ELEMENTS	Nesting material	Shelter
	During spring, twiggy branches and foliage provide nest-building materials. Some foliage, such as yarrow and fleabane leaves, are insecticidal and kill parasites to protect young chicks.	Plant foliage provides shelter for birds to protect them from predators (*see pp.102–105*). Foliage also often attracts insects, giving birds a source of food, too.

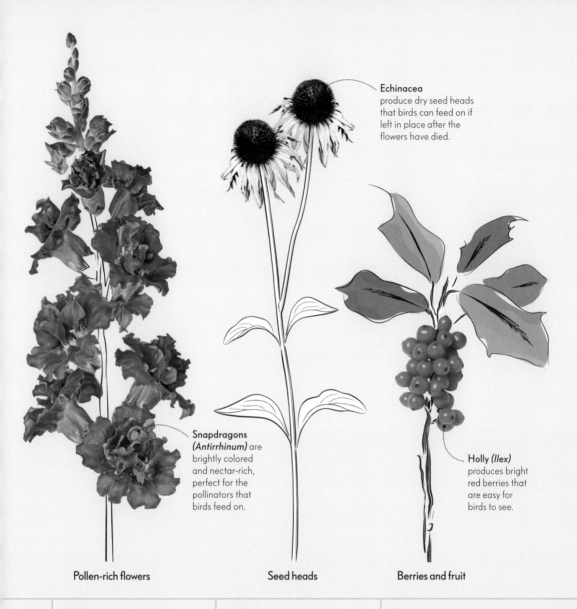

Echinacea produce dry seed heads that birds can feed on if left in place after the flowers have died.

Snapdragons (Antirrhinum) are brightly colored and nectar-rich, perfect for the pollinators that birds feed on.

Holly (Ilex) produces bright red berries that are easy for birds to see.

Pollen-rich flowers

Seed heads

Berries and fruit

Insects

Bright, nectar-rich flowers attract a variety of pollinators and other insects, which are a vital food source for birds as they feed their newly hatched young (*see pp.106–109*).

Seeds

The seeds in seed heads are another key source of food for birds (*see pp.114–117*). Many seeds will be available throughout the winter, long after other fruits and berries have been eaten.

Fruit

Fruit- or berry-bearing plants provide seasonal sources of food (*see pp.110–113*). Birds are attracted to berries with bright colors—often red or orange that contrast with green foliage.

LAYERING PLANTS TO CREATE NATURAL SHELTER

To make the most of your space, be it small or large, layer your plants to create shelter, food opportunities, and a more varied habitat for birds.

Planting in layers replicates how plants organize themselves naturally so they can gain enough sunlight and avoid competing too much with similar plants. A layered planting design also creates natural shelter pockets within your garden or borders, or even within a group of containers, so that your birds can safely explore without risk of being spotted by predators. Layering is also an attractive way to plant, providing interest at different heights and different times of year.

The three layers

First, start by thinking about incorporating a tree or two into your design. These need to be at the back or edge of your yard. If you don't have a lot of space, grow a small tree in a container: try crab apple, cherry, and olive trees, which will provide good shelter for birds with their foliage as well as some food when they fruit. You can even consider neighboring trees as your tallest layer if you don't have any space.

The trees you have will influence what you can grow underneath. Those with large or dense foliage, such as oaks, provide a lot of shade so you will need to select shade-loving plants such

as foxglove, primrose, and lungwort for your lowest layer. Trees such as the paperbark maple (*Acer griseum*) allow more sunlight to get through the foliage, so there is a much wider selection of plants available to grow underneath.

Next, create a shrub layer. These give a year-round structure to the garden with their woody twigs and branches, and provide enough shelter to make birds feel safe. They ideally need to be situated further into a border, or toward the back if the border is against a wall or fence. You could also include a few shrubs in the center of a group of containers, to achieve the same effect.

The lowest layer consists of annual or perennial flowering plants and ground cover. Place smaller plants, such as primroses, in the front of a border, with taller flowering plants, such as lavender, tulips, and sunflowers, behind.

Final additions

Position any food sources (see pp.58–61) where there is shelter to retreat to, but also enough open space to watch for predators. The optimum place is near where the shrubs meet the tree layer. If you do not have a tree, then near to your taller flowers and shrubs is ideal.

Trees

Plant trees near the back of your border, or if you don't have space, factor in a tree in a neighboring yard as the tallest layer. Birds will use trees as perching spots on their way to your shrubby layer and the rest of your yard and feeders. Tree flowers are also very important for pollinating insects, which in turn provide a food source for birds (*see pp.106–107*).

Shrubs

Planted toward the back of a border, shrubs allow sunlight through to the plants below. To fit more shrubs into a small space, plant them against a wall or fence (either in the ground or in a container) and train them up a trellis to cover the vertical space. They provide shelter for birds when foraging, a safe place to perch to feed their young, and a point from which to dart to and fro when they are visiting your bird feeders.

Flowers

Plant smaller flowers near the front of a border or group of containers and taller flowers throughout your space. This gives the smaller plants the best chance of receiving sunlight, while also providing shelter to invertebrates.

PERFECT PLANTS: SHELTER

Shrubs make an ideal refuge for birds. Choosing the right variety for your container or garden need not be difficult, whether you are starting from scratch or choosing a new one to fill in a gap.

Spotted laurel (*Aucuba*)

One of the hardiest shrubs, this is great for nesting birds.

Foliage type: evergreen, dense.

Suitable for: shade; any soil type.

Camellia (*Camellia*)

Birds feed on insects attracted to the shrub's vivid blooms.

Foliage type: evergreen, open.

Suitable for: partial shade; well-drained, slightly acidic soil.

Rhododendron 'Daphnoides'

Large purple flowers in late spring attract butterflies.

Foliage: evergreen, dense.

Suitable for: sun or partial shade; moist, well-drained soil.

Lavender (*Lavandula*)

Offers good ground cover and is ideal for pollinators.

Foliage: evergreen, mixture of open and dense.

Suitable for: sun or partial shade; dry soil.

Elderberry (*Sambucus nigra*)

Elderberries provide food for visiting birds in fall.
Foliage: deciduous, open.
Suitable for: sun; well-drained soil; cooler climate.

Kousa dogwood *(Cornus kousa)*

Ideal for late-nesting birds including pigeons and doves.
Foliage: deciduous, open.
Suitable for: sun or partial shade; moist soil.

Weigela (*Weigela*)

Strong pollen and scented flowers in late spring and early summer attract many pollinators for birds to feed upon.
Foliage: deciduous, dense.
Suitable for: sun or partial shade; moist soil.

Spiraea japonica 'Goldflame'

Low-growing shrub, suitable for containers. Ideal for pollinators with nectar-rich summer flowers.
Foliage: deciduous, dense.
Suitable for: sun or partial shade; any soil type.

EVERGREEN SHRUBS

These shrubs provide shelter for birds all year as they do not lose their foliage in fall. During the winter they are a relatively warm, safe roosting place, especially if you choose a shrub with dense foliage such as a rhododendron (*see opposite*). Evergreens also offer security when small birds are feeding in the open—the birds can flit from shrub to feeder and back.

DECIDUOUS SHRUBS

These shrubs produce new foliage and flowers during the spring and summer, which often attract pollinating insects that birds feast upon. In fall their leaves drop—but not before putting on a show by turning vivid colors. At the same time, the shrubs' berries provide additional food for birds.

ATTRACTING POLLINATING INSECTS

Flowering plants provide nectar for pollinators, such as bees, hoverflies, butterflies, and moths, which birds then feed on in turn.

Pollinators visit flowers in search of nectar to eat. In their quest for nectar they transfer pollen from plant to plant, a process that will result in the production of seeds and fruit later in the year, making them a valuable part of our ecosystem.

Many bird species feed on pollinating insects: some catch them as they fly from flower to flower, while others seek them out during earlier stages of the insects' development (at the larval or caterpillar stage, for instance) in order to feed them to their young. Warblers, flycatchers, and thrushes in particular look for flying insects and insect larvae to feed upon.

SPACE SAVERS

Pots and containers are perfect for spaces where planting is difficult, such as balconies or patio gardens. Fill them with flowering plants or vines if you can offer support in the form or a trellis or frame of sticks in the pot. You can also plant climbing plants in pots that hook on to balcony edges so the plant will drape downward rather than climbing up.

Choosing a variety of plants

When choosing plants to attract pollinators, make sure to include a variety of flowers that open at different times. Many flowers stay open day and night, attracting a variety of pollinators, including butterflies and moths, around the clock. A few night-blooming plants offer evening scent for both the gardener and night-flying pollinators such as moths, providing a source of food for both bats and night-hunting birds.

Make sure to plant seasonally, too, with plenty of floral variety throughout the year. By planting a mix of early- and late-season flowers, you can provide a reliable source of nectar to pollinators at times when feeding opportunities might otherwise be scarce.

Including flowering plants that grow to different heights in your garden will also help you attract as many pollinating insects as possible. A mixture of tall- and short-stemmed plants will give some pollinators shelter from predators while allowing enough to be available for your birds to enjoy.

Birds

The greater the number of flying insects your yard can attract, the more likely it is that you'll be able to attract the likes of warblers, swallows, swifts, and the aptly named flycatchers as they hunt for food in the air, or feed on caterpillars and other young insects in and among your plants.

Insects

Bees, butterflies, moths, hoverflies, and a range of other flying insects will make the most of the flowers you provide. Some insects, such as ladybugs, green lacewings, or praying mantis, may create a home in your yard, or lay eggs on certain plants.

Flowers

Provide a nectar-rich array of flowering plants, ideally in a mixture of different colors and varieties (see *opposite*). The more flowers you can offer throughout the year (with your borders and containers, with mini-meadows, or even through your choice of trees and shrubs), the greater a foundation you'll be able to offer to support your garden food chain.

PERFECT PLANTS: NECTAR-RICH FLOWERS

A mix of day- and night-flowering border plants and vines can encourage pollinators to linger in your yard—and attract birds looking to feed upon them.

Butterfly bush (*Buddleja*)
This heavily scented plant is the best choice for butterflies, which flock to the blooms in large numbers. **Type:** day-flowering border plant.

Woods' rose (*Rosa woodsii*)
The open faces of these flowers gives butterflies and bees easy access to perch and feed upon the nectar. **Type:** day-flowering climbing plant.

Foxglove (*Digitalis*)
Richly scented and easy to grow, with tall flower heads that allow insects to easily find and access the nectar. **Type:** day-flowering border plant.

Honeysuckle (*Lonicera*)
Ideal for small spaces as it can be trained up a trellis or fence, honeysuckle is a great choice for attracting bees. **Type:** day-flowering climbing plant.

Evening primrose (*Oenothera*)
The beautiful scent and open faces of evening primrose flowers often attract hawkmoths, among other species.
Type: night-flowering border plant.

Night gladiolus (*Gladiolus tristis*)
A great option if you have gaps in your planting to fill in, with tunnel-like flowers that suit smaller moth species.
Type: night-flowering border plant.

American wisteria (*Wisteria frutescens*)
A statement for borders and containers. The showy, fragrant blue and purple petals attract bees and birds.
Type: day-flowering climbing plant.

Garden phlox (*Phlox paniculata* 'Logan Black')
Phlox come in multiple varieties. Their bright, fragrant flowers attract hummingbirds and pollinators.
Type: day-flowering border plant.

Night-blooming jasmine (*Cestrum nocturnum*)
Easy to train up a fence or trellis, with small flowers that can attract a large number of different moth species.
Type: night-flowering climbing plant.

PROVIDING FRUITS AND BERRIES

Traditional fruit trees and bushes provide food for both birds and humans.

Fruits and berries are produced by the flowers of certain plants following pollination, and give visiting birds a chance to use their natural foraging behavior of hopping around the branches seeking food. They are a highly nutritious source of food at a time birds need it most, either to get through the winter or to sustain them on migration.

For gardeners, berries and fruits provide a pop of color during the fall and winter months, and it's interesting to watch birds visiting to feast on the fruit. Many berries are perfect for birds but are poisonous for us to eat; check it's safe before trying anything unfamiliar.

Plant berry-bearing shrubs in borders or in pots. To fit even more in, some can be trained to grow up trellises on fences and walls. As for fruit trees, if space is limited, choose a variety that is grown on a dwarfing rootstock; this controls the vigor of the tree, limiting its growth. Look for M27 rootstock, which will grow to 6 ft (1.8 m), or M9, which will grow to 8 ft (2.4 m); both are suitable for a small garden or a large container.

Virginia creeper berries appear in clusters in winter and are eaten by woodpeckers, titmice, chickadees, thrushes, and catbirds. Its mid-summer flowers offer nectar and pollen to many bee species.

The large, colorful hips of *Rosa rugosa*, often used to make beautiful and robust hedges, are a favorite of robins, cedar waxwings, and hermit thrushes.

Tufted titmouse

Hermit thrush

Birds will strip red currants as they ripen, so cover the bush with temporary netting. Remove it once you have harvested as many as you need, and leave the rest for the birds.

Winter berries

Many trees and shrubs produce berries and fruits in fall that last through winter. Some roses produce hips that are loved by birds. These winter fruits and berries are a vital source of calories; the more winter calories birds consume, the likelier that spring breeding season will be successful. Birds naturally aid in the distribution of seeds as the indigestible seeds inside fruits come out in their droppings.

Summer fruits

You can grow your own fruits in a container, on a balcony, in a small vegetable patch, or interspersed among flowers and shrubs in a mixed border. Gardeners often place nets over soft fruit bushes such as black currants and raspberries to prevent the birds eating the fruits; consider netting them, harvesting what you need, then sharing the rest with the birds. Strawberries are simple to grow in containers. Raspberries and red currants will also grow in containers but are much hungrier, needing a larger pot and feeding; raspberries will also need the support of a trellis, or wires on a wall.

American robin

Strawberries grow well in containers, and if you keep picking them they can produce for a long time. Consider growing a container of strawberries for the birds.

PERFECT PLANTS: FRUITS AND BERRIES

The trees and shrubs shown here provide a wide selection of fruits and berries for birds to enjoy at different times of the year.

Cherry (*Prunus* spp.)

Self-fertile varieties produce fruit alone, while others need a compatible tree nearby to fruit; check before buying.
Fruits: dark red or black cherries in summer.

Crab apple (*Malus sargentii*)

Cedar waxwings, American robins, eastern towhees, and gray catbirds compete for the fruits.
Fruits: small apples in fall and winter.

Cockspur hawthorn (*Crataegus crus-galli*)

This thorny, ragged shrub's berries are devoured by cedar waxwings, northern cardinals, and gray catbirds.
Fruits: red berries in winter.

Rowan (*Sorbus aucuparia*)

Pollinators enjoy this tree's delicate white summer flowers; waxwings, grosbeaks, and finches feed on its berries.
Fruits: bundles of red berries in fall and winter.

Raspberry (*Rubus* spp.)

Easy to grow near a wall or fence, raspberry bushes are loved by towhees, sparrows, and finches.
Fruits: summer- and fall-fruiting types are available.

Holly (*Ilex* spp.)

With its dense, evergreen foliage, holly offers valuable winter shelter, while its berries are loved by birds.
Fruits: bright red berries appear in winter.

Guelder rose (*Viburnum opulus*)

Thrushes, finches, and waxwings feast on the berries that appear within this shrub's colorful fall foliage.
Fruits: bright red berries in fall.

Blackberry (*Rubus* spp.)

Some gardeners dislike wild blackberries (also known as brambles), but their thorny growth provides refuge for birds.
Fruits: black fruits in summer.

PROVIDING SEEDS FOR BIRDS

Harvesting the seeds of plants in your own garden provides an inexpensive alternative to store-bought bird feed.

By growing a variety of flowering plants in addition to stocking a feeding station with a selection of food mixes (see pp.42–45), you can diversify the range of food sources your yard can offer birds.

An American goldfinch uses its specialized thin beak to extract ripe seeds from this dried seed head.

Hardy annuals which grow and flower in one year, are particularly good plants to raise for seed. Getting started is straightforward: you can easily buy seed, but if you can, consider using a local seed swap, as this will allow you to find seeds that thrive in your area (potentially including some unusual varieties), which will have a greater chance of appealing to your local bird population.

You can sow hardy annuals in weed-free soil where they are to flower, or sow them into pots then transplant them out into their final growing place when they have a number of healthy leaves. Keep them watered so they don't dry out, and dispose of any weaker seedlings to give the strongest plants enough space to thrive.

After flowering, your plants will produce seed heads. At this stage you can leave them be if you wish; some birds, including goldfinches, feed directly from certain seed heads (see *left*). Alternatively, you can harvest seed for feed (see *opposite*). If you do leave your plants alone, the seeds will often disperse themselves and self-sow nearby. Over time this may create a wildflower area in your garden, where seeds are sown naturally.

To harvest sunflower seeds, cut off the flower head and allow it to dry fully. Rake out the seeds with your hands, separating them from the chaff before storing.

Turn old yogurt containers into pots for your seedlings by adding a few drainage holes and filling them with compost.

Harvesting seeds

If you want to collect seeds to use in your bird seed mixes, keep an eye on the plant from which you want to harvest. A very rough guide is that seeds are ready to harvest around two months after flowering, when the flower changes color to a duller, brownish shade.

On a dry day, go out and cut off the seed heads or flower heads you want to harvest, then place them in a paper bag so that any seeds that fall out are not lost. Spread them out on paper towel on a tray in a warm area such as a kitchen, near a radiator, or in a sunny windowsill. Check them often as the flower heads dry, ready for harvesting. Some larger seed varieties, such as sunflower seed (see left), can be easily harvested from the flower, while others, such as thistles, may require you to pick the seed out of the seed pockets using tweezers. Clean off any non-seed material to prevent mold, then store the harvested seeds in labeled paper envelopes in a cool, dark place.

Using harvested seed

Depending on the quality of the harvested seed, you may choose to resow it the following year or to use it as feed. If the adult plant you harvested the seed from was healthy and the seed looks good, it should be perfect to resow in another container or in the ground; otherwise, include it in your bird food mixes.

Sunflowers, thistle, millet, and milo can be grown specifically for harvesting for bird food. With these plants, you can harvest some of these seeds and leave others on the plants for birds to feed on naturally.

PERFECT PLANTS: SEEDS

Whether you want to harvest seed for bird feed or simply sow pollinator-friendly wildflowers, these plants are all easy to grow from seed.

Thistle (*Cirsium*)
After the plant flowers during summer, the seeds can be harvested and added to fine seed mixes for finches.
Ideal for: harvesting seed or leaving for birds to eat.

Sunflower (*Helianthus*)
Sunflower seeds are incredibly versatile and are perfect for seed mixes or to leave for birds to feed naturally.
Ideal for: harvesting seed or leaving for birds to eat.

Milo (*Sorghum bicolor*)
Easy to harvest, milo seeds can be added to ground feeders or classic mixes (*see p.45*).
Ideal for: harvesting seed or leaving for birds to eat.

Bachelor button (*Centaurea cyanus*)
As well as being great for pollinators, birds will pick at bachelor button seeds after the plant finishes flowering.
Ideal for: harvesting seed or leaving for birds to eat.

Sweet pea (*Lathyrus odoratus*)
A versatile, pollinator-friendly flower that isn't fussy about where it grows, sweet pea is ideal for planting in pots.
Ideal for: harvesting seed or leaving for birds to eat.

Foxglove (*Digitalis*)
Loved by both pollinators and nectar-feeding birds, like hummingbirds. The seeds are easy to remove and resow.
Ideal for: harvesting seed or leaving for birds to eat.

Dahlia
Birds will pick at the seed heads of dahlias after they have flowered. The seeds can also be added to mixes.
Ideal for: harvesting seed or leaving for birds to eat.

HOW TO MAKE SEED BOMBS

Seed bombs are fun for adults and children alike, and help create natural pockets of flowers that support visiting wildlife.

A seed bomb is essentially a mixture of seeds combined with potting mix and a binding agent, then rolled to form a ball. While you can use a packet seed mix, it's a great idea to use seeds you've harvested from the plants in your garden (*see pp.114–115*), as they'll be more likely to successfully germinate. The seeds of wildflowers, annuals, perennials (particularly spring- and fall-flowering varieties) are all good options.

To use the seed bomb, simply throw it onto soil where you want the seeds to grow, then either water it in so that the ball begins to soften, or leave it to naturally fall apart and disperse its seeds.

You can also buy premade seed bombs in a biodegradable packaging; these naturally decay over time, releasing the seeds. Although seed bombs are fine to leave where they land, you can also thin out the seedlings as they grow.

YOU WILL NEED:

• 1 cup of seeds
• 5 cups of potting mix
• 2–3 cups of clay powder or soil

1. Select your seeds
Choose a mixture of varieties: small plants, stand-out feature flowers, and bushier plants either harvested from your garden or bought.

2. Add the potting mix

Add the potting mix to the seed mixture, adding a small amount of water to help them bind together.

3. Use a binding agent

Add a little clay powder or soil to the mixture. This acts as a binding agent, helping ensure that your ball does not fall apart when it's dry.

4. Shape into a seed bomb

Form the mixture into balls and leave them in a cool, dry place to harden.

5. Go wild!

Throw your seed bombs onto patches of bare soil in your yard.

WATER FOR BIRDS

WATER FOR BIRDS

Providing water in your yard allows birds to drink and bathe there. If you add a pond, the water can also draw in a huge variety of other wildlife, much of which is beneficial for birds. You are starting to create a more complex ecosystem in which birds and other wildlife will thrive.

Nashville warblers and other migrants bathe in shallow areas of ponds, birdbaths, and puddles to refresh themselves.

WATER IN THE LANDSCAPE

Water is essential for birds' survival. It offers them not only food and drink, but also a way to keep themselves clean.

Adding water to your landscape introduces a whole new habitat, opening up your yard to a host of different wildlife. A dedicated birdbath (*see pp.126–127*) will attract and support birds, or, if you have space, you could make a pond (*see pp.134–137*). A pond allows you to grow plants that like water and boggy conditions; these in turn attract insects that may be food for birds.

Drink

During hot spells, in areas where water is hard to come by, or in winter when puddles are iced over, birds turn to yards for water in ponds, birdbaths, and dishes. Birds can drink water from plants and dew, but a clean, accessible water source in your yard is just as vital as food and nesting sites. Birds that feed on seeds gain little moisture from their food, so they need more water than insect eaters. Place your birdbath and especially your pond carefully as birds weigh the risks of predation against the need to drink. The safer the water appears to be, the more likely birds are to use it.

Food

Having a water source in your yard, such as a pond of any size, means you are indirectly

Extra food for birds
Plants in and around the pond attract insects to pollinate flowers or lay eggs; some birds will come to feed on these insects, their eggs, and their larvae.

Swallow

Water in the landscape is vital for birds but also for insects and small mammals. A yard that has water attracts a much more diverse range of wildlife than one without.

providing food for birds. Insect-eating birds will love the many insects and larvae that live in or near a pond; insects often arrive as soon as a pond is made. Frogs and toads will appear; they benefit your yard by eating slugs, but they are also potential food for birds of prey such as owls, which use ponds to hunt for amphibians and small mammals to feed upon.

Bathing

Most birds use puddles and shallow birdbaths to bathe, splashing and showering themselves with water in order to naturally remove parasites and bacteria. Water helps soften debris stuck to their feathers, making it easier for birds to preen (which involves using their beak to clean and smooth each feather).

Blue jay

Black-capped chickadee

Hanging birdbath
A shallow dish suspended from a tree offers a safe environment for birds to bathe and drink.

Shallow area
A shallow, gently sloping area at the edge of the pond allows birds to bathe and drink safely.

CHOOSING AND POSITIONING A BIRDBATH

The best birdbath suits your landscape style and space. Place it where birds will feel safe and, if possible, where you can see it, too.

Birdbaths come in many styles from formal to rustic. They can also be at different levels, raised off the ground or at ground level. You can create your own birdbath, either by making one (*see pp.128–129*) or by putting out a shallow dish.

Raised bath

Typically on a metal or concrete pedestal, these baths are ideal for smaller birds that like to bathe together, such as sparrows or robins, or for more nervous species that use baths but

A reliable drinking spot is needed, especially in very hot or freezing weather, but is often used all year.

may need a quick escape route, such as chickadees and wrens. They make an attractive focal point in a border or on a lawn.

Hanging birdbath

Another type of raised birdbath is a hanging dish of water that you can suspend from a tree or a bracket on a fence, or fit around a freestanding pole. Often these are made of plastic so they are light, and have rough sides so birds can grip the surface. If you are hanging your birdbath from a tree, avoid those that shed lots of blossoms or fruits.

Ground-level bath

Birdbaths that are near or on the ground come in a variety of shapes and sizes. Larger baths are ideal for birds such as thrushes, grackles, and doves, which can walk in, and sometimes they double up as shallow mini-ponds for toads and frogs or as a drinking source for rabbits. If you have a pond, you could have a shallow area at one side to make a ground-level bathing spot for birds. For any ground-level bath, ensure there is an easy way out for small mammals that find their way into it, either a slope on one side or stones piled up to enable them to climb out.

Water depth

Shallow baths, up to 2 in (5 cm) deep, are mainly for smaller species with shorter legs as these tend to dip their toes into the water and sit down to bathe. Deeper baths are ideal for larger backyard birds, but also for species such as hawks. Ensure a deeper bath has sloping sides so birds and other animals can climb out.

A simple dish of clean water on the ground or placed on a low surface such as a wall is all most birds need for a bath.

Where to place your birdbath

When bathing, birds can be vulnerable to predators, and they will enjoy their bath more if they feel safe. Position your birdbath where birds can see around them; if it is very near trees and bushes, birds might avoid it for fear of predators, although they may appreciate some cover a little further away to retreat to. For a pedestal-style bath in a border, you could grow thorny plants underneath, or put thorny clippings among surrounding vegetation so cats don't approach the bath. For a raised bath, you need to ensure it is stable and on level ground so it will not topple. If birds are not using the bath, try a different location to see which the birds prefer. Avoid placing the bath near feeders as some of the food is likely to end up in the bath, making the water dirty.

MAKE YOUR OWN BIRDBATH

*A number of household items can be adapted
to make a small water feature that is safe
for birds to use.*

For your birdbath, choose items that will hold water, or that can be made watertight. Select the size depending on the space available. Possible candidates are tires, plastic storage boxes, dish tubs, or trash can lids; ensure there are no sharp edges. Adjust the depth by using stones inside and out as platforms for birds to stand on. A tire, as shown here, takes a little more work to make into a birdbath, but will become a more permanent feature.

1. Make a hole for your bath
Dig a wide and shallow hole where you want your birdbath to go, measuring the hole against the tire as you dig to make sure it's the right size.

2. Mold soil around the tire
Place the tire inside the hole and mold the soil so it covers the inside edges of the bottom of the tire. You can vary the soil levels within the tire to make shallower areas.

3. Make your tire watertight

Cover the tire and soil inside and around it with plastic sheeting or a tarpaulin, pushing it down into the shape of the tire. Build up the soil around the outside of the tire to hold the sheeting in place.

4. Finish your birdbath

Add some stones to the edge of the tire to help it blend in to the surroundings. Place stones of different sizes inside the tire as platforms for birds to stand on while bathing or drinking, and to help them grip. Add water.

ALTERNATIVE DIY BIRDBATHS

Use a dish tub, digging it halfway into the surrounding soil. Place stones in and around it.

A plastic storage box with stones inside and out provides places for birds and mammals to sit while they drink.

Place a trash can lid on some bricks or stones so it is stable, then add some stone perches in the water.

TAKING CARE OF YOUR BIRDBATH

Make sure you carry out a few simple tasks to keep your birdbath clean and ready for birds throughout the year.

Depending on the season, there are different jobs to do to maintain your birdbath in the best condition, and to ensure that birds are safe from bacteria and diseases. Just adding water to your birdbath or relying on rainfall to fill it up is not enough.

SPRING AND SUMMER

Top off the water
Make it part of your daily routine to check on your birdbath and top it off with fresh water so there is plenty for bathing and drinking. In summer the water evaporates particularly quickly.

Remove debris
Sometimes there is a buildup of leaves, petals, droppings, and other debris in the birdbath. These can be a nuisance when birds are trying to bathe, so scoop these out regularly.

Clean and remove algae
Freshwater algae frequently contaminates a birdbath, so don't allow it to build up. It can get onto birds' feathers, sticking them together. It's also slippery. Empty your bath regularly and clean it with a brush, warm water, and a little soap before refilling it with clean water.

FALL AND WINTER

Keep the water fresh

In the fall and winter, clean, shallow water can become scarce. Often smaller drinking holes become flooded or frozen, meaning there is a lack of natural water to bathe and drink from. Change the water every day or two to keep it fresh, and dump it out and scrub the inside of the bath regularly.

Provide a way out for wildlife

Ice, algae, and leaves can all build up during the fall and winter months and small birds and mammals can get stuck in the bath, unable to climb up the sides. Provide a rough wooden ramp to help creatures climb out. If you come across a bird or mammal that is stuck, put on some gloves and remove it, allowing it to sit nearby and dry off naturally.

Prevent water freezing solid

To stop ice from building up in the birdbath, float a tennis ball in the water; it may be moved around by the wind and will keep a tiny patch open. Pouring warm (not too hot) water into the birdbath will melt a small area of ice. Where temperatures are below freezing for much of the winter, consider a specialized heated birdbath or place an immersible water heater into the bath. Be sure to monitor water levels and add water as needed.

WHY HAVE A POND?

Even the smallest wildlife pond offers riches to birds and other wildlife, and provides a wonderful focus in your landscape.

Water attracts amphibians, insects, and other invertebrates as well as small mammals. Some birds feed on these directly; others use the pond for bathing and drinking. The plants and creatures live together and form an ecosystem both above and below the surface. Whatever size pond you're able to create (see pp.134–137), you'll be providing a thriving space for wildlife.

Having a pond enables you to plant a range of water and bog plants that you would otherwise not be able to have in your yard. Some plants keep the water healthy and provide a habitat for water creatures; others offer nectar or a place for insects to lay eggs. A pond needs different depths to accommodate a variety of plants. Some are suited to the middle, and need to be planted in deep water; others are for the shallower edges; others float in the water. Plants suited to boggy conditions can go around the edges, providing shelter for chipmunks, frogs, and toads, as well as for birds.

Sustenance for birds

Dragonflies, caddis flies, and many other insects visit ponds and lay their eggs there. Bats may swoop down to catch insects. Over time, newts will appear, along with frogs and toads; they use ponds to breed in, and shelter in a shady spot in the yard for much of the year. It's essential to have a shallow, sloping edge in at least one part of the pond so it's easy for amphibians, birds, and small mammals to climb into and out of the pond.

Having an additional ecosystem with more diverse wildlife provides a number of new feeding opportunities for birds. Swallows and martins may swoop down to feed from bigger ponds, while warblers and chickadees visit small ponds in search of insects. A pond may also attract birds that are not typically seen in yards, such as herons or ducks. A shallow area with a platform for bathing means that a pond can also double as a birdbath and water source.

Benefits for people

A pond in your yard is not just good for wildlife and birds, but it can help your well-being and mental health. The sound of water is often associated with feelings of tranquility and relaxation. You have a space to watch wildlife act naturally, as you get to know the population of plants and wildlife below the surface. Insects that interact with your pond are equally fascinating, such as pond skaters and water boatmen on the surface, and aerobatic dragonflies and damselflies darting above and around the water. A pond through the seasons adds a different dimension to your yard from a frosty, silent pool in winter to the activity of frog eggs and tadpoles in spring, followed by flowers buzzing with insects in summer.

SAFETY AROUND PONDS

Children are fascinated by ponds and the wildlife within, but you need to be aware of the risks and help children use and visit your pond safely. Always supervise children near a pond, and talk to them about safety. Encourage them to kneel by a pond so they are less likely to fall in. For very young children, start with a tiny pond (see pp.134–135), and wait before making a larger one, or consider fencing off the pond.

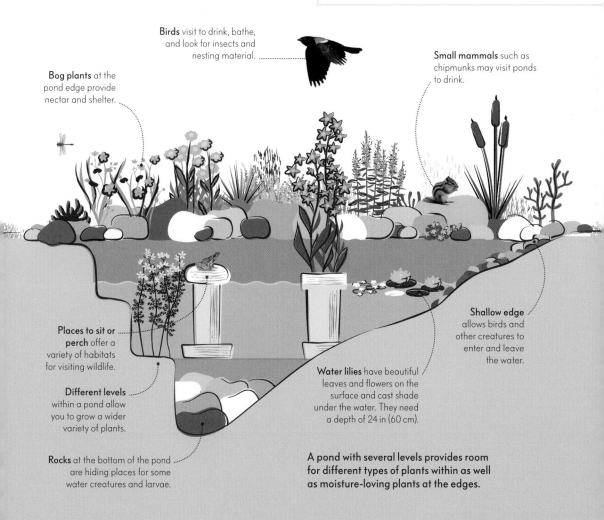

Birds visit to drink, bathe, and look for insects and nesting material.

Small mammals such as chipmunks may visit ponds to drink.

Bog plants at the pond edge provide nectar and shelter.

Places to sit or perch offer a variety of habitats for visiting wildlife.

Different levels within a pond allow you to grow a wider variety of plants.

Rocks at the bottom of the pond are hiding places for some water creatures and larvae.

Water lilies have beautiful leaves and flowers on the surface and cast shade under the water. They need a depth of 24 in (60 cm).

Shallow edge allows birds and other creatures to enter and leave the water.

A pond with several levels provides room for different types of plants within as well as moisture-loving plants at the edges.

MAKE YOUR OWN SMALL POND

*A tiny pond works well in a small yard or even
on a balcony, and is safe for children
to make and watch.*

Invertebrates in particular will thrive in a tiny pond. Birds can feed from the visiting insects and, if you provide a perch such as a large stone next to the pond, birds can also drink from it. You can create small ponds by adapting items such as dish tubs or large plant pots. Reuse an old fish tank to create an outdoor pond with an educational aspect as children (and adults) can see through the sides to watch what's going on under the water. When designing even the smallest pond, try to include a range of habitats such as hiding spots under the water, and plants to create shelter and provide food. In a small pond it's most practical if your vessel is half-filled with plants so you can see down through the surface to the bottom.

1. Line the vessel

Begin by lining the bottom of your vessel with a mixture of soil designed for water gardens and some small stones. Aim for a depth of 2 in (5 cm) so the soil is deep enough for plants.

2. Create a way out

Add stones up the side that will offer a way in or out for wildlife. Place a half plant pot or a piece of bark to create shelter for shier species such as newts, and invertebrates such as caddis fly larvae.

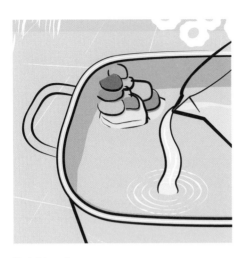

3. Add water

If you have rainwater available from a water barrel, this is best to use. Pour the water slowly from a pitcher or watering can so your stones and soil are not dislodged. Fill to just below the lip of the vessel.

4. Add plants

Plant some plugs or cuttings of aquatic plants such as yellow flag iris, water lily, or frogbit into the soil or in mesh baskets lowered into the water. Two or three plants is enough, positioned in corners.

5. Introduce wild creatures

If you can acquire a little pond water from a friend or family member, pour it in—it is likely to contain larvae or small invertebrates. If not, wild creatures usually find a new pond quickly, starting with insects that fly in. Animals that thrive are often smaller ones such as water fleas, caddis fly larvae, mayflies, and snails.

MAKE YOUR OWN LARGE POND

Adapt your pond's shape and size to the space you have available. Try to include a variety of habitats for plants, birds, and other wildlife.

First choose a site for your pond; it will be a key feature for many years, so ensure you are happy with its location. An open space with plenty of natural light is ideal. Avoid choosing a spot close to trees, as falling leaves can rot in the water and cause problems. Using a flexible pond liner allows you to create any size or shape of pond, including a more natural shape that suits the space you have. When digging the hole for the liner, take great care to include the essential elements of a wildlife pond, such as a sloping gradient, a shallow area for birds to bathe in, and different depths for planting different types of water plant (*see pp.138–139 for more ideas*).

1. Mark and dig your pond shape
Using a spade to cut the soil, mark the shape and size of the pond you want. Choose whether you want a slope for a deeper zone in your pond, and how many levels to have. When you are happy with the shape, dig it out and create the levels.

2. Line the pond
After digging out your pond, firm down the base by walking over and over it. Add some soft soil or sand to line the base of the area, and ensure there are no sharp stones as these could puncture your liner. Add the liner, smooth it carefully, and mold it to the shape of your pond.

3. Add a base of soil and stones

Add water garden soil to the bottom of your lined pond, with stones in a variety of sizes. The soil is for planting, and the stones will provide refuge for some of the bottom-dwelling species.

4. Fill your pond with water

Add water from a hose. Allow it to settle for a week or so—initially it will look cloudy, but it will clear. Tuck the edge of the liner firmly into the natural grass line around the pond to hold it in place.

5. Plant water plants

Add some plants. Use some habitat plants, such as yellow flag iris, and some deep water plants, such as water lilies, in a mesh basket. Place stones to alter the levels at the edges and give access for wildlife. Use slabs or bog plants to disguise the liner edge.

ADDING PLACES FOR WILDLIFE

Plants are the key to creating different habitats for wildlife within and around a pond.

Together, plants and water creatures (*see pp.140–141*) help establish a balance in your pond, keeping the water fresh and clear. If you use different plant types, and if your pond provides access, food, and places for creatures to shelter, you will build a healthy ecosystem of plants and wildlife.

Plants for wildlife

The better the water quality, the more life you will have in your pond. Harmful algae multiply when they have lots of sunlight and nutrients, but you can use pond plants to reduce sunlight and nutrient levels. Oxygenating plants help balance nutrients in the water, absorbing any excess. Plants that float or have floating leaves make a shady habitat underwater. Aim to have 50 percent of the surface covered with plants to reduce levels of sunlight.

Marginal and bog-loving plants provide natural shelter for wildlife. Birds and mammals use these for nesting; warblers, for example, weave the long stems of marginals into their nests. Edge plants give a safe, damp place for invertebrates to breed. Pond invertebrates such as nematodes and aquatic worms (*see p.140*) feed on decaying matter at the bottom of the pond, preventing it from building up.

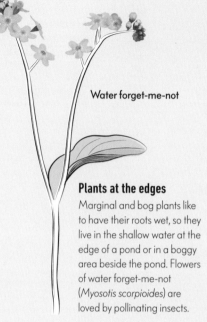

Water forget-me-not

Plants at the edges

Marginal and bog plants like to have their roots wet, so they live in the shallow water at the edge of a pond or in a boggy area beside the pond. Flowers of water forget-me-not (*Myosotis scorpioides*) are loved by pollinating insects.

Water lily

Deep water plants

Adding deep water plants such as water lilies (*Nymphaea*) breaks up the surface of the water and offers shade during the summer months. The flowers provide food for pollinators.

Hornwort foliage
is submerged
under the water.

Floating plants

Add floating plants, such as frogbit
(*Limnobium spongia*), to create a
shady habitat underwater. Hornwort
(*Ceratophyllum demersum*) is a
free-floating oxygenator, helping
keep the water clear.

Hornwort

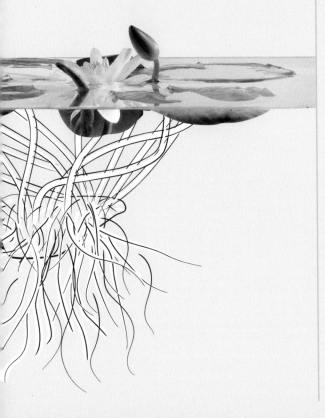

HELPING WILDLIFE IN YOUR POND

Drinking pool

Place some pebbles to one side of your
pond, just breaking the surface of the water,
creating a shallow area for birds to bathe in
and drink from.

Toad house

Add a toad house to the foliage at the edge of
your pond for frogs and toads to use for shelter
from predators. It provides cool shade in
summer and protection from cold in winter.

Ladder

Make a "ladder" to one side of your pond out
of wood or stepping stones so birds, frogs, and
newts can climb out; this will also help small
mammals who may fall in.

POND CREATURES

A pond builds up a balanced ecosystem of creatures that live in and around the water. All contribute to keeping the pond healthy, and some are food for birds.

Fathead minnow

Fathead minnows are native to most of North America and are common baitfish. They are also excellent pond fish, tolerant of a wide range of water conditions. They feed on mosquito larvae as well as algae and decaying vegetation. They help keep your pond clean.

Frogs

These amphibians do not spend all their life in the water and often find somewhere damp to go such as a toad house (*see p.139*) or under a nearby rock. In the water, they feed on the flies that lay their eggs in the pond, and they lay their spawn.

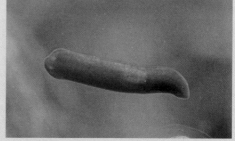

Water hog-lice

Abundant within ponds, these absorb oxygen through their shells. Found on the bottom of the pond, they feed upon decaying matter and plants.

Flatworms

Common in ponds, and ranging in size and color, flatworms live on the bottom of the pond. Their colors mean they are well camouflaged and hard to see.

Diving beetles

Larvae of diving beetles are one of the largest predators within a pond. They spend time in all parts of the pond and return to the surface to breathe.

Damselflies and dragonflies

These beautiful insects drop their eggs into the water for the young to grow. The predatory larvae eventually climb on to plant stems, emerging to become adults.

Caddis fly larvae

These larvae live underwater and have a sticky silk-like material around their bodies, to which they attach items for camouflage. You can usually see what vegetation is at the bottom of the pond depending on what is on their casings. They feed upon plants.

Newts

Newts spend their time hidden within the vegetation of a pond and feed upon flies, larvae, and smaller invertebrates. In summer, they come out of the water to bask somewhere warm such as on a rock in the sun. They lay their spawn in the water.

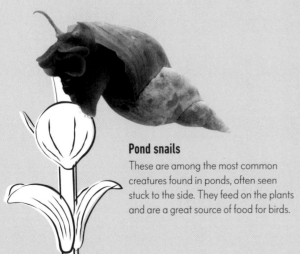

OTHER POND CREATURES

- Toads
- Snakes
- Turtles
- Bats
- Mayflies
- Mosquitoes
- Pond skaters
- Water beetles
- Bloodworms
- Freshwater shrimp

Pond snails

These are among the most common creatures found in ponds, often seen stuck to the side. They feed on the plants and are a great source of food for birds.

MAINTAINING YOUR POND

Make the most of your pond by doing some regular, basic maintenance to keep the water and habitats in good shape.

Full-sized lakes and large ponds create an ecosystem of their own, which can more or less maintain itself. A backyard pond, however, can become filled with overgrown plants, or too many fallen leaves, leading to fewer and less varied creatures, and lower water quality. You needn't empty the pond or remove the wildlife and habitats, but instead you can make slight alterations over the course of the year, and improve the quality of the water and the pond environment for wildlife.

Spring and summer maintenance

During the spring and summer months, use a small net to fish out debris such as fallen leaves. If left, they will rot, adding too many nutrients to the water and reducing its quality.

Birds are very useful at transporting tiny invertebrates between ponds on their feet and beaks, but they also spread algae and unwanted plants. Keep an eye on the algae and plant growth within your pond; when algae is becoming noticeable, pull it out by hand or by

Cut off any decaying leaves (*see left*) or vegetation as you notice them. When algae starts to build up, remove it with a stick or rake (*see above*).

Top off water levels as needed (*see left*). In fall, the simplest method to gather leaves is to put a net over the pond (*see below*); otherwise collect leaves regularly so they don't build up.

twisting a stick around to gather it. Place any plants and algae removed from your pond on the side for a few days before discarding it to allow sheltering pond creatures to escape.

Low water levels can cause issues during the summer as the water evaporates quickly. Keep your pond at a level to fill your drinking and bird bathing area and to cover your plants. A water marker makes it easier for you to monitor when the level is dropping. Top off using a garden hose.

If the water level is going down very quickly, check that you do not have a leak in the liner. If you suspect a leak, wait until the water has stopped draining and search for the hole at that level, marking it with chalk once you find it. Repair the liner with an aquatic patch. Allow the patch to bond to the liner then top off the water.

Fall and winter maintenance

In the fall, ponds can fill with debris from trees shedding their leaves and seeds, which will affect the water quality if they are allowed to collect and then decay. A net secured over the pond stops the leaves falling in. Remove the net and shake out the leaves from time to time.

Check regularly as temperatures start to drop, and crack or remove any buildup of ice. If your pond will completely freeze over in winter, consider installing a deicer to keep the water circulating, preventing it from freezing over.

MAINTAINING A SMALL POND

With a smaller pond, especially in a container, maintenance is particularly important as one aspect out of balance can affect the whole pond. Ensure your plants are healthy and happy and cut out any stems that spread too much. Promptly remove any leaves, and top off the water as needed. Regularly check your water quality. If it looks too murky, then remove any decaying vegetation in the bottom of the pond.

KEEPING
BIRDS SAFE

KEEPING BIRDS SAFE

It's important to have an awareness of some of the risks to birds. From natural and pet predators to common bird diseases, you can take steps to reduce or minimize these threats. Your yard will become a safer place for birds to visit, and they will feel secure enough to spend time there.

Cats are among the main predators of birds in the yard, but with some management you can reduce their hunting opportunities.

PEST PREVENTION

Discourage unwelcome backyard visitors by making sure your feeding stations are not easy food sources for pests.

Squirrels, chipmunks, raccoons, and mice can be attracted to feeders where food is readily available, especially if it is a ground feeder. One of the best ways to discourage them is to stop the supply of food for a while, then resume feeding and watch for their return. Likewise, if squirrels are targeting a certain feeder, take it down for a while. If a lot of food is being spilled, this can also attract rodents; secure a plastic dish under the feeder to catch fallen seed.

Using shrubs as a barrier

A perfectly natural way of discouraging predators such as cats from stalking your feeding station is to use plants as barriers, particularly shrubs. Thorny bushes such as roses and brambles have benefits to insects and pollinators and can prevent predators from reaching or pouncing at the base of the feeding station.

Using feeder guards

Cage guards around feeders prevent larger bird species, rodents, cats, foxes, and squirrels from feeding or stalking the birds. For poles up to a table or feeding station, use a baffle that looks like an upside-down bowl to prevent squirrels and mice from climbing up the pole.

Hanging feeders from trees

Squirrels and other pests may take advantage of a feeder hung from a tree branch; if you think this may become an issue, position your feeders well away from trees, beyond any squirrels' reach. Alternatively, try hanging your feeders up using thin string, such as trimmer line—this is slippery and hard for rodents to climb down.

DEALING WITH INSECT PESTS

Gardeners are used to dealing with unwanted visitors on their plants, but some pest-prevention practices harm birds. Avoid insecticides and inorganic chemical solutions, which can poison the whole backyard food chain (*see p.107*); slug pellets, for example, hurt birds if they eat a poisoned slug. Copper tape around pots or crushed eggshell around plants help deter slugs without harming the yard's ecosystem.

HOW TO MANAGE CATS

Sometimes cats can cause issues with wildlife and birds in the yard, but there are ways of minimizing your cat's threat to wildlife.

While there are a number of reasons why bird population numbers are in decline, one factor that you may be able to control is the behavior of your pet cat. Cats are thought to kill millions of birds and small mammals each year, and while it is thought that cats kill birds that are already weak, it's nevertheless worth minimizing feline opportunities to hunt birds. These suggestions may help reduce the damage your cat could potentially cause, and defend your feeders against cats from neighboring yards.

Deterring cats

- Feed your cat around the same time as you feed your birds; this will ensure the cat is well fed before it goes outside.
- To give birds a chance to feed undisturbed, don't let your cat outside for an hour before sunset and an hour after sunrise; this allows birds to feed at the beginning and end of the day.
- Build up the plants around your bird feeders with thornier varieties, including roses. This creates a barrier that may discourage cats from approaching too closely.
- If you have unwanted cats from neighboring yards, spread citrus peel and zest near your bird feeders and dishes because the smell may deter them. You can also buy cat deterrent devices, which emit a high-pitched sound disliked by cats but inaudible to people.

A bell on a cat's collar warns birds and small mammals that something is approaching and gives them time to hide.

Avoid placing nest boxes too near vegetation or places where cats can obtain easy access. This box is very unlikely to be used.

Scaring away birds

Putting a collar on a cat with a bell on it will warn birds that a predator is approaching. Ensure the collar fits snugly but has a quick release should your cat get tangled in a hedge or undergrowth.

Neutering

Consider having your cat neutered or spayed. In addition to avoiding any unwanted kittens, this may help some backyard birds as the cat typically will not wander too far from the yard.

HOW TO IDENTIFY DISEASES IN BACKYARD BIRDS

Despite our best efforts, not all yards and bird feeders are kept clean, and diseases can spread when birds visit different feeders.

Taking care to clean your bird feeders (*see pp.64–65*) and birdbaths (*see pp.130–131*) regularly will remove bacteria and help stop diseases spreading from bird to bird. There are several diseases to watch out for, though they can be hard to spot.

Trichomoniasis

This is the most common illness found in finches, doves, and pigeons—although it can affect any bird species. It does not affect humans or mammals. Trichomoniasis causes lesions on the throat, making it harder for the bird to swallow its food over time. Signs of this disease typically come in the form of labored breathing, and finches look very wet even in dry weather. The disease is spread through the bird regurgitating its food, which contains the disease particles, onto surfaces such as bird tables where other birds can come into contact with it. It can also spread via birdbaths. Ensure you clean your birdbaths and bird feeders regularly and thoroughly.

Clean feeders thoroughly. It is best to do this outside using a bucket, brush, and gloves set aside for the purpose to prevent any cross-contamination.

American goldfinches are susceptible to avian pox, which causes skin lesions, often next to the eyes or beak, but also on legs or wings.

Avian pox

This is a skin infection that appears in the form of growths, particularly around the head, legs, and wings, with more appearing over time. Birds typically behave normally with the most affected being wild turkeys, finches, and doves. The disease is spread through bird-to-bird contact and indirectly through contact with contaminated areas such as bird feeders. Ensure feeders are cleaned thoroughly with extra scrubbing on the perches.

Salmonellosis

A bacterial infection, this is hard to detect and has few symptoms. Birds may show signs of general ill-health, being lethargic, hanging around feeders, and not responding to danger. Infection is spread through droppings, thus regular cleaning of nest boxes, bird feeders, and birdbaths is paramount.

Mycoplasmal conjunctivitis

This is commonly known as "house finch disease" because it principally affects house finches. Affected birds have swollen, red eyes that may be runny or crusty. This affects their ability to see, feed, and protect themselves from predators. Sick birds may contaminate seeds at a feeder, which may be spread to healthy birds.

House finches are most commonly affected by mycoplasmal conjunctivitis, which causes eyes to swell and become encrusted.

BIRD
PROFILES

BIRD PROFILES

In this section you will find information about 56 birds you may see in your yard. Some are common visitors, some occasional or seasonal ones. The profiles will help you identify the birds you see and find out more about their habits, their songs and calls, and where they feed, nest, and shelter.

Bird feeders can give you a front-row seat for observing birds up close, and learning to identify them.

AMERICAN KESTREL
Falco sparverius

Size 9–12 in (22–31 cm) long; 20–24 in (50–60 cm) wingspan; 4 oz (117 g).

ID features Smallest falcon in North America. Both sexes have crowns, white cheeks with 2 dark vertical markings, and buffy underparts. Tails and pointed wings are long and barred. Males have blue-gray wings, rusty backs and tails; females and juveniles have rusty backs and wings. Legs are yellow with short toes for diving into tall grass to capture prey. Beaks are short and sharp.

Distribution Widespread in semi-open country throughout the US, northern Canada, and into Mexico and the Caribbean. Only northernmost birds migrate south during winter.

Call Has 3 different calls: shrill "klee-klee-klee" when excited, a "chitter" during courtship, and a "whine" during feeding.

Habitat Open country, grasslands, farm fields.

Feeding Solitary daytime hunter. Looks for prey while perched on utility wires or fence posts. Hovers over potential prey on rapidly beating wings before plunging to the ground to capture them. Eats mostly large insects, but also small mammals, reptiles, and birds.

Nesting Pair bonds seek nest sites in holes or cavities in trees, rock crevices, or nest boxes. Do not excavate their own cavities or use nesting materials. Breed April–June; produce 1 brood of 4–6 eggs; incubate 26–32 days; fledge at 28–32 days.

Plants Prefers areas with short vegetation and few trees.

Water Dietary water obtained through prey. Bathes in standing water or rain showers.

SHARP-SHINNED HAWK
Accipiter striatus

Size 10–14 in (25–34 cm) long; 21–26 in (53–65 cm) wingspan; 5 oz (140 g).

ID features Smallest hawk of North America. Sexes similar; females ⅓ larger than males. Long tail; short, rounded wings; small, round head. Blue-gray crown and back, light belly with rust-colored barring, darkly barred tail squared at tip. Long yellow legs and feet with needlelike talons. Short, sharply hooked beak.

Distribution Widespread from northern Canada to Gulf states. Winter in southern US, Mexico, and Central America.

Call Usually quiet, except during nesting season when there is active vocalization between pairs.

Habitat Prefers dense, coniferous or mixed hardwood stands when breeding. Found at forest edges or backyards in winter.

Feeding Ambushes songbirds in flight or while on feeders. Brings prey to a plucking post and removes feathers before eating it. Eats mostly birds, but also mice, voles, and large insects.

Nesting Breeding season March–June. Both sexes gather nest materials; female builds the platform-style nest. Produce 1 brood of 3–5 eggs; incubate 21–35 days; fledge at 21–32 days.

Plants Nesting material of coniferous sticks, twigs, bark, or grass.

Water Dietary water needs obtained from prey.

EASTERN SCREECH OWL
Megascops asio

Size 6–10 in (15–25 cm) long; 18–22 in (45–56 cm) wingspan; 6 oz (180 g).

ID features Small, stocky, short tail, broad wings with feather mottling. Round head with yellow eyes, prominent ear tufts. Two color morphs: gray or reddish-brown. Legs and feet are strong and feathered. Talons long and sharp to penetrate vital organs. Beak is gray-green, short, and hooked at tip for gripping and tearing prey.

Distribution Widespread throughout the US east of the Rocky Mountains and into southern Canada. Nonmigratory.

Call Usually a tremulous whinnying, resembling a horse, or a monotone trill lasting a few seconds.

Habitat Adapted to mixed-deciduous forests, mature orchards, rural woodlands, and urban yards and parks.

Feeding Solitary nocturnal hunter of open woodlands from perches. Pounces feet-first to capture diet of insects, earthworms, reptiles, amphibians, rodents, and small birds, often eating them whole. Regurgitates pellets of undigested bones, fur, and feathers.

Nesting Sexes pair bond for life. Nest in natural cavities, holes made by woodpeckers, or nesting boxes. Do not build their own nests or use nesting materials. Breed March–May; produce 1 brood of 3–5 eggs; incubate 26–34 days; fledge at 26–31 days.

Plants Roosts in tree cavities, dense foliage, or on branch next to tree trunk.

Water Fulfills water needs from prey but may drink and bathe in ponds and birdbaths.

MOURNING DOVE
Zenaida macroura

Size 9–13½ in (23–34 cm) long; 5½–6 in (14–15 cm) wingspan; 5 oz (150 g).

ID features Sexes similar. Soft gray-brown back and wings; long, pointed tail; buffy underparts. Black spots on wings; wings produce a soft whistling noise when flushed. Small, round head; black spot on side of face. Short reddish legs and feet. Thin, dark straight bill.

Distribution Most common yard bird in North America. Found throughout the continental US and southern Canada. Northernmost birds migrate.

Call Readily recognized by its mournful cooing.

Habitat Adapted to several habitats including open country, farmland, parks, roadsides, and backyards. Commonly perches on utility wires.

Feeding Ground feeds almost exclusively on seeds, occasionally snails. Bill is soft so it swallows seeds whole. Once crop is filled it quickly retires to a roost to digest its meal. Eats grit to assist digestion.

Nesting Prolific breeders. Pairs for life. Nests in trees or shrubs on flimsy platforms lined by twigs, grass, or pine needles. Both parents share incubation and feeding of young. Breed February–October; produce up to 6 broods of 2 eggs; incubate 14 days; fledge at 14 days.

Plants Avoids dense forests and swamps. Eats sunflower seeds, corn, millet, and weed seeds.

Water Uniquely able to sip water. Prefers freshwater sources that are vegetation-free.

SWIFTS FAMILY
CHIMNEY SWIFT
Chaetura pelagica

Size 4½–6 in (12–15 cm) long; 11–12 in (27–30 cm) wingspan; ¾ oz (21 g).

ID features Sooty gray plumage all around. Cigar-shaped body; long, slender, pointed wings; stubby, squared-off tail; very short legs. Looks like a "flying cigar." Unable to perch, but strong feet and sharp claws enable it to cling to vertical surfaces, assisted by pointed tips on tail feathers. Black, very short beak, but large mouth that opens wide for capturing insects in flight.

Distribution Widespread in cities and towns over eastern US and southeastern Canada. Migrates in winter to South America.

Call Consists of a rapid, high-pitched series of sharp twittering chirps.

Habitat Feeds in areas with abundant flying insects. Not a forest dweller.

Feeding Eats flying insects while in flight itself. Often forage in small flocks.

Nesting Pair-bond mates break twigs in flight from branches for use in building nests almost exclusively in chimneys. Parents build a shallow bracket-style nest of twigs held together by sticky saliva to the inside surface of a chimney. Parents incubate eggs and feed their young regurgitated insects. Produce 1 brood of 4–5 eggs; incubate 19–21 days; fledge in 28–30 days.

Plants Apart from nesting materials, do not rely much on vegetation.

Water Skilled at taking sips of water and bathing from surface of a body of water.

HUMMINGBIRDS FAMILY
RUBY-THROATED HUMMINGBIRD
Archilochus colubris

Size 3–3½ in (7–9 cm) long; 3–4¼ in (8–11 cm) wingspan; ³⁄₂₀ oz (4.3 g).

ID features Metallic green upperparts, gray-white underparts, black wings. Males have ruby-red throats and forked tails; females have blunt tails. Rapidly beating wings produce low-pitched hum. Able to suddenly stop; hover; and move forward, backward, up, and down. Very small legs and feet preclude walking or hopping but can perch on branches. Long, straight bills for probing flowers.

Distribution Only breeding hummingbird in the eastern half of the US and southern Canada. Migrates to Central America.

Call Buzzy chase call drives off intruders.

Habitat Mixed woodlands, forest edges, meadows, gardens, parks, and suburban neighborhoods.

Feeding Feeds on nectar, spiders, and tiny insects from the air or from spiderwebs. Enters torpor on cold nights to conserve energy.

Nesting Male present only during courtship and mating. Female builds walnut-sized nest of bud scales on a tree branch or in a shrub; outside is covered with lichens or moss; inside lined with plant down, reinforced by spider silk. Breed April–September; produce 1–2 broods of 2 eggs; incubate 12–14 days; fledge at 18–23 days.

Plants Feeds on nectar from wildflowers, shrubs, and vines. Strongly attracted to red or orange colors.

Water Daily water needs provided by nectar and insects. Bathes in shallow edges of streams, pools, or birdbaths.

RED-BELLIED WOODPECKER
Melanerpes carolinus

Size 9–10½ in (23–27 cm) long; 15–18 in (38–46 cm) wingspan; 2½ oz (70 g).

ID features Both sexes colorful with black and white zebra-striped backs and wings; pale gray-brown bellies with an obscure reddish patch on lower belly (hence, its name). Males have a reddish crown and nape; females lack the crown. Dark gray legs and strong feet; pairs of toes face front and back, which, with stiff tail feathers, allows bird to hitch up trees. Stout, chisel-like black bill.

Distribution Found throughout eastern US and southern Canada. Largely nonmigratory.

Call Very vocal during breeding season; both sexes give a rolling "chr, chr, chrchrchr" call and drum.

Habitat Highly adaptable. Found in deciduous or mixed pine forests, wet forest lowlands, and suburban parks and yards.

Feeding Uses sticky tongue to pull food out of tree crevices; gleans beetles, other insects, acorns, fruit, nuts, and seeds. Frequent visitor to feeders.

Nesting Excavate nest cavities in dead trees, snags, fence posts, or use nest boxes. Breed May-August; produce 1–3 broods of 4–5 eggs; incubate 12–14 days; fledge at 24–26 days.

Plants Lines nest cavities with wood chips. Eats mainly vegetable matter in the fall and winter.

Water Gets most water from diet. Drinks and bathes where water has collected, or at birdbaths.

DOWNY WOODPECKER
Picoides pubescens

Size 6–7 in (15–18 cm) long; 10–12 in (25–30 cm) wingspan; 1¹⁄₁₆ oz (30 g).

ID features Smallest woodpecker in North America. Sexes alike. Black upperparts, tail; white back, throat, and belly; white spots on black wings. Male has red patch on back of head; absent in female. Strong feet have two toes facing forward, two facing backward; used with stiff tail feathers to hitch up tree trunks. Short forcepslike bill for gleaning.

Distribution Year-round resident throughout most of the US and Alaska and Canada.

Call Uses a short, high-pitched "pik" call, a "kee, kee-kee-kee" rattle call, and nonvocal drumming with bill to attract mates or defend territories.

Habitat Deciduous woodlands, wooded areas near streams, city parks, and suburban backyards.

Feeding Principally ants, beetles, and pest insects from live and dead trees, or larvae in plant galls. Also fruits, berries, and seeds. Likes suet, shelled peanuts, and black oil sunflower seeds from backyard feeders.

Nesting Monogamous pairs excavate nest cavity in dead limbs. Breed May–July; produce 1 brood of 4–5 eggs; incubate 12 days; fledge at 20–25 days.

Plants Openings of nest cavities are camouflaged by lichen and fungus; cavities lined by wood chips.

Water Drinks and bathes from water collected on branches, streams, shallow ponds, or birdbaths.

WOODPECKERS FAMILY
HAIRY WOODPECKER
Picoides villosus

Size 9–10 in (23–26 cm) long; 15–16 in (38–41 cm) wingspan; 2½ oz (70 g).

ID features Looks like a larger version of the downy woodpecker but having a larger bill. Only males have a red patch on back of head. Strong feet with sharp claws, used with stiff tail feathers to hitch up tree trunks and limbs. Straight, chisel-like bill for chipping bark to capture insects.

Distribution Found throughout North America, most of Canada, and into Mexico. Largely nonmigratory.

Call Give a sharp, explosive "peek" call or belted kingfisher–like rattle call. Uses nonvocal drumming to attract a potential mate or defend its territories.

Habitat Mature deciduous and mixed coniferous forests, forest edges, parkland, suburban backyards. Found together with downy woodpeckers, but is shier.

Feeding Mostly insects foraged from larger trees. Also nuts, seeds, fruit, and suet from feeders.

Nesting Monogamous breeders excavate nest cavities in live or dead trees. Breed May–July; produce 1 brood of 3–6 eggs; incubate 11–12 days; fledge at 28–30 days.

Plants Nest cavities lined only with wood chips. About 20 percent of diet is vegetable matter.

Water Gets most of its liquid needs from diet. Drinks and bathes from water collected in branches of trees, puddles, or shallow streams. Not a frequent visitor to birdbaths.

WOODPECKERS FAMILY
NORTHERN FLICKER
Colaptes auratus

Size 11–14 in (28–36 cm) long; 17–21 in (42–54 cm) wingspan; 4½ oz (128 g).

ID features Distinctively patterned plumage. Gray-brown with black barring on back and wings; white rump; underbelly light, spotted black with black patch across chest. Males have black or red cheek stripes, reflecting two common subspecies. Yellow or red coloration on undersurface of wings. Strong legs and feet for hopping on ground and perching on thin horizontal branches. Long, slightly downcurved bill.

Distribution Found throughout North America and into Central America. Largely migratory.

Call Several communications: single, sharp "kyeer" call; a lengthy "ki ki ki ki" rattle call; drums on tree trunks or metal objects to attract mates or declare territories.

Habitat Open woodlands, mountain forests, marsh edges, city parks, suburban backyards.

Feeding Principally ground feeders. Avidly hammers ground with bill to access ant colonies and beetle larvae, using long, sticky tongue to lap them up.

Nesting Monogamous pairs excavate cavities in dead trees or limbs. Breed March–July; produce 1–2 broods of 6–8 eggs; incubate for 11–13 days (shared); fledge at 25–28 days.

Plants Nests only lined by wood chips. Eats poison ivy and oak berries, elderberries, sumac, and sunflower seeds in winter.

Water Drinks and bathes from shallow streams, knotholes in trees, and occasionally at birdbaths.

SWALLOWS FAMILY
TREE SWALLOW
Tachycineta bicolor

Size 5–6 in (13–15 cm) long; 12–14 in (30–35 cm) wingspan; ¾ oz (21 g).

ID features Agile, acrobatic fliers with bright white underparts and steely-blue (males) and duller brownish-blue (females) upperparts; broad or slightly notched tails. Tiny reddish-brown legs and feet. Small, short bills; wide mouths for scooping up insects in flight.

Distribution Northern two-thirds of US, Alaska, and Canada. Migrate in winter to southern US, Mexico, and Central America.

Call Male sings a musical gurgle. Pairs use up to 14 calls to communicate to mates, young, or intruders.

Habitat A social bird that prefers open wooded areas near water (marshes, swamps) that provide nesting sites and abundant flying insects.

Feeding In summer, actively forages morning to evening capturing flies, beetles, and winged ants over bodies of water and meadows; in winter, eats bayberries, fruit, and plant seeds.

Nesting Often return to same areas to breed. Their small bill and feet make them dependent on preexisting holes or cavities in dead trees for nests; also nest in bluebird houses. Breed May–July; produce 1 brood of 4–7 eggs; incubate 14–15 days; fledge at 18–22 days.

Plants Female lines nest with plant material, pine needles, moss, and feathers.

Water Drinks and bathes by skimming over and contacting surface of water with their beak or body.

SWALLOWS FAMILY
BARN SWALLOW
Hirundo rustica

Size 6½–7½ in (17–19 cm) long; 12½–13½ in (32–34½ cm) wingspan; ¾ oz (21 g).

ID features Male has deep blue upperparts; a rusty forehead, chin, and throat; and buffy underparts that are separated by a dark blue breast band. Females are slightly duller. Wings are long and pointed; tails are long and deeply forked. Short, black legs and feet for perching on wires and bare branches. Triangular, wide-gaped bills for capturing insects in flight and collecting mouthfuls of mud during nest building.

Distribution Widespread across most of North America. Migrates in winter to South America.

Call Song is a cheerful warble. Uses several vocalizations for different situations. Uses bill to make a clacking sound.

Habitat Prefers open country, pastureland, and suburban parks, especially near water and man-made structures (barns, stables, bridges, houses, utility wires).

Feeding Forages on insects (flies, beetles, moths, wasps) in flight.

Nesting Adults construct cup-shaped nests on man-made structures using mud pellets carried in their beaks; nests lined with grass, feathers. Both feed young. Breed May–August; produce 1–2 broods of 4–5 eggs; incubate for 13–17 days; fledge at 18–23 days.

Plants Uses bare branches for perching and grass for lining nests.

Water Drinks by scooping up water with its open mouth while skimming over a surface of water. Touches water surface with its breast when bathing.

SWALLOWS FAMILY
PURPLE MARTIN
Progne subis

Size 7–8 in (18–20 cm) long; 15–16 in (38–41 cm) wingspan; 2 oz (56 g).

ID features Largest North American swallow. Adult male is uniformly dark bluish-black; female has a gray-brown forehead, throat, and belly. Both have long wings and slightly forked tails. Legs and feet are short but strong. Sharp toenails are used to move them up and down in tight nesting spaces. Bills are broad and flat with wide gapes for catching flying insects.

Distribution Found over eastern US and central Canada with limited locations in western US. Winter in South America.

Call Very vocal. Uses gurgling croaks, chortles, and rolling rattles for mating, feeding, warning, and teaching young to fly.

Habitat Open country, towns, and meadows near water. Perches on power lines to rest and preen.

Feeding Catches insects (wasps, moths, dragonflies, butterflies, winged ants, flies, mosquitoes) in flight.

Nesting Except for western species, martins almost exclusively use man-made martin houses placed near open water. Breed in colonies and create nests of vegetation and mud. Breed April–August; produce 1 brood of 4–6 eggs; incubate 15–18 days; fledge at 26–32 days.

Plants Western located birds use abandoned woodpecker nests in trees or saguaro cactus.

Water Bathes in the rain or by striking belly against water it flies over; drinks by skimming surface of pond and scooping up water with its lower bill.

WRENS FAMILY
HOUSE WREN
Troglodytes aedon

Size 4½–5 in (11–13 cm) long; 6–7 in (15–16½ cm) wingspan; ⅜ oz (11 g).

ID features Sexes similar in coloration. Warm brown upperparts, paler throat, and grayish underparts. Faint barring on short, rounded wings and frequently cocked tail. Relatively large feet for grasping onto perches. Narrow head and thin bill for probing crevices for prey.

Distribution Found throughout the US and southern Canada. Migrates to the southern US and Mexico for winter.

Call Delivers an energetic stuttering, but bubbly series of sounds that indicate their presence. Both sexes sing. Active, but secretive.

Habitat Often found near human settlements where there is dense shrubbery, thickets, brush piles, or lush gardens for protection and food sources.

Feeding Forages in gardens or dense tangles on common insects, butterfly larvae, caterpillars, spiders, or snails.

Nesting Secondary cavity nesters in old woodpecker holes, natural crevices, or nest boxes. Males build several "dummy" nests of small, dry twigs. A female selects the nest she likes and completes construction of a cup-shaped nest lined with moss, fur, pine needles, or feathers. Breed April–July; produce 1–2 broods of 5–8 eggs; incubate 12–15 days; fledge at 15–17 days.

Plants Adding trees, bushes, and shrubs to the yard attracts these birds.

Water Drinks and bathes from birdbaths.

WAXWINGS FAMILY
BOHEMIAN WAXWING
Bombycilla garrulus

Size 7½–9 in (19–23 cm) long; 12½–14 in (32–36 cm) wingspan; 2 oz (56 g).

ID features Sexes look alike. Soft grayish plumage overall; black wings bear white and yellow patches; short tail ends in bright yellow band, rusty orange undertail; black face and chin; pointed crest. Legs and feet are short, but strong for perching. Bills are short and broad to aid foraging of berries, which they swallow whole.

Distribution Resident in subarctic areas of Alaska and western Canada.

Call No true song. Flocks are vocal, communicating with high-pitched "sirrrr" trills.

Habitat Breeds in open boreal forests near wetlands. In winter, large nomadic flocks migrate into northern regions of US in search of fruit.

Feeding Flies out from an open perch to catch insects in summer. Eats fruit and berries throughout the year. Roams in large flocks (with cedar waxwings and American robins) in winter; descends on fruit-bearing trees or shrubs.

Nesting Nests built near trunk of trees or in shrubs. A cup of small twigs lined with soft vegetation, feathers, or fur. Breed June–July; produce 1 brood of 4–6 eggs; incubate 13–14 days (by female; both parents feed); fledge at 14–16 days.

Plants Enjoys berries of mountain ash, juniper, holly, and crab apples.

Water Largely obtains its water from the fruit it eats. In winter, will eat snow.

WAXWINGS FAMILY
CEDAR WAXWING
Bombycilla cedrorum

Size 6–7 in (15–18 cm) long; 9–12 in (23–30 cm) wingspan; 1¼ oz (35 g).

ID features Similar in appearance to its Bohemian waxwing cousin, but smaller. Soft brownish-gray upperparts, yellowish belly with white undertail. Black facial mask and chin; yellow terminal band on tail; red waxlike wing tips. An acrobatic forager, often hangs upside down using strong grayish-black legs and feet to reach a cluster of berries, which it plucks and rips into with its short, wide bill.

Distribution Found across southern Canada and northern US. A social bird that, in winter, migrates in tight flocks in search of fruit as far south as Mexico and South America.

Call A high-pitched, wheezy whistle, "tre-e-e-e-e," used for communicating with members of a flock.

Habitat Breeds in open wooded areas, orchards, golf courses, urban and suburban parks, near water.

Feeding Eats insects and fruit in summer; roams in search of tree-bearing fruit and berries in the winter. Swallows berries whole.

Nesting Females build a cup-shaped nest in a fork of tree branches and line with grass, fine roots, moss, or fur. Breed June–August; produce 1–2 broods of 3–5 eggs; incubate 11–13 days; fledge at 14–18 days.

Plants Likes berries from dogwood, serviceberry, winterberry, and juniper plants.

Water Attracted to sound of water. Drinks and bathes from shallow creeks or in birdbaths.

THRUSHES FAMILY
AMERICAN ROBIN
Turdus migratorius

Size 8–11 in (20–28 cm) long; 12–16 in (30–41 cm) wingspan; 2⅝ oz (75 g).

ID features Large, plump songbird. Males identified by their reddish orange breast, dark gray head and tail with bright white corners, dark streaks on white throat. Females are duller. Long dark legs, feet for perching and running and hopping across lawns. Stout yellow bills with dark tips are plunged into the ground to capture earthworms or to pluck berries.

Distribution Found throughout North America. Most migrate in winter to the Gulf Coast and into Mexico.

Call Song is a rich carol that rises and falls with a pause before it is repeated. Can be heard at first dawn and before nightfall.

Habitat Deciduous forests, parks, urban and suburban yards.

Feeding Forages on lawns or grassy areas for earthworms, caterpillars, beetle grubs; eats fruit and berries in winter.

Nesting Female builds open cup nest of vegetative matter, twigs, feathers, paper, reinforced by mud located on horizontal branch or man-made ledge. Breed April–July; produce 2–3 broods of 3–5 eggs; incubate 12–14 days; fledge at 14–16 days.

Plants Uses plant materials for its nest; eats crab apples, cherries, blueberries, mulberries, and honeysuckle berries.

Water Fruit provides most of its water needs; will also drink and bathe from standing pools of water or birdbaths.

THRUSHES FAMILY
VEERY
Catharus fuscescens

Size 6½–7¼ in (16–18 cm) long; 11–11½ in (28–29 cm) wingspan; 1½ oz (42 g).

ID features Sexes look alike. A plump bird with reddish brown upperparts, buffy throat and breast with indistinct brownish spotting, white underbelly with grayish flanks. Round head with gray cheeks. Pink legs and feet. Short, thin bill.

Distribution Found across southern Canada and northern US. Long distance migrant to Brazil in winter.

Call Sings a reedy sound at dawn and dusk consisting of a series of downward spiraling "veer" notes, like its name.

Habitat Wet deciduous woods of spruce, fir, oak, maple, or aspen with dense understory; willow or alder thickets; trees near swamps.

Feeding Takes long hops and uses bill to turn over leaves in search of caterpillars, beetles, spiders, and snails. Eats berries and fruit after breeding season.

Nesting Female builds cup-shaped nest of leaves, weeds, bark, roots, and moss near or on the ground. Breed May–July; produce 1–2 broods of 3–5 eggs; incubate 10–14 days; fledge at 10–12 days.

Plants Readily eats juneberries, strawberries, blackberries, blueberries, wild cherry, and wild grape.

Water Drinks and bathes in shallow streams or pools of water.

THRUSHES FAMILY
SWAINSON'S THRUSH
Catharus ustulatus

Size 6½–7½ in (16–19 cm) long; 11½–12 in (29–31 cm) wingspan; 1 oz (28 g).

ID features Exists in two subspecies: olive-backed (Eastern range) and russet-backed (Pacific Coast range). The more numerous Eastern forms have olive-brown upperparts; long wings; white belly; buffy colored eye ring, cheeks, and throat; with distinct dark spots on upper breast. Short pink legs and feet for foraging within trees. Short, straight bill.

Distribution Breeds in coniferous forests with dense understory in northern North America and in wet deciduous woodlands in Pacific states. Visits all types of woodlands providing dense shrubbery during migration. Migrates to Central and South America.

Call Song is a breezy, flutelike, upward-spiraling chorus like the veery, but with a rising pitch.

Habitat Shy, secretive bird. Seeks wet thickets of willow or alder for cover and access to insects.

Feeding Forages on the ground or along tree branches for beetles, ants, caterpillars, moths, or grasshoppers during breeding season. Eats berries at other times.

Nesting Builds open cup nest of twigs, decayed leaves, moss, lichens, bark, and mud near trunk of tree. Breed April–July; produce 1–2 broods of 3–4 eggs; incubate 12–14 days; fledge at 10–14 days.

Plants Eats raspberries, elderberries, blackberries, and sumac.

Water Drinks and bathes from shallow streams or ground-level birdbaths.

THRUSHES FAMILY
HERMIT THRUSH
Catharus guttatus

Size 6–7 in (15–18 cm) long; 10–11 in (25–28 cm) wingspan; 1 oz (28 g).

ID features Sexes look alike. There are several subspecies that differ geographically and in coloration. Upperparts are olive-brown to gray-brown; distinct white eye ring; white underparts with grayish flanks; throat and breast sport dark spots. Distinguished from other thrushes by its reddish tail, which it frequently flicks up and lowers slowly. Has pink legs and feet, and a short, straight bill.

Distribution Breeds in brushy understories of mixed coniferous-deciduous forests from Alaska and Canada into northeastern and western US. Migrates in winter to southern US and Central America.

Call Songs are piercing, flutelike, and repetitive with different pitches.

Habitat Frequent visitors to wooded areas (urban and suburban parks, trails, pond edges) with dense shrubbery for protection and access to insect and berry sources and water.

Feeding Hops on forest floor lifting leaves with its bill and uses its feet to shake grass in search of insects. Eats fruits and berries throughout the year.

Nesting Females construct a cuplike nest low in a tree or shrub. Breed May–July; produce 1–2 broods of 3–5 eggs; incubate 11–13 days; fledge at 10–15 days.

Plants Nest materials include grasses, moss, pine needles, catkins. Eats grapes, serviceberries, elderberries, other berries in winter.

Water Drinks and bathes near shaded streams or ground-level birdbaths.

THRUSHES FAMILY
EASTERN BLUEBIRD
Sialia sialis

Size 6–8 in (15–20 cm) long; 10–13 in (25–33 cm) wingspan; 1¹⁄₁₆ oz (30 g).

ID features Adult males have bright blue upperparts and tail; rusty red throat, breast, and flanks; and round, white belly. Females are duller with gray upperparts. Short black legs and feet. Bill is slender and straight.

Distribution Eastern North America to Gulf states. Partial migrant, depending on weather and food availability. Some move south into Mexico in winter.

Call A musical "churr-wi" phrase made by both sexes for communication and coordinating behaviors.

Habitat Very social bird that prefers open country, wooded areas with little ground cover, roadsides, orchards, parks. Often perches on wires or fence posts before swooping down to capture an insect.

Feeding Gleans insects (grasshoppers, crickets, beetles, moths, caterpillars) from the ground or plants in summer; eats fruit or berries in winter.

Nesting Secondary cavity nesters because their beaks and feet are not strong enough to create their own. Uses old woodpecker holes or man-made bluebird houses. Female builds cuplike nest of twigs lined with grass, feathers, hair. Breed February–September; produce 2 broods of 3–7 eggs; incubate 13–16 days; fledge at 15–20 days.

Plants Seeks blueberries, dogwood berries, wild grape, black cherry, sumac in winter.

Water Drinks and bathes from birdbaths or sources of running water (ponds, streams).

VIREOS FAMILY
RED-EYED VIREO
Vireo olivaceus

Size 5–5½ in (13–14 cm) long; 9–10 in (23–25 cm) wingspan; ⅝ oz (17 g).

ID features Sexes alike. Long, slender birds with olive-green upperparts, white underparts. Lacks wing bars. Has black-edged gray crown, white eyebrow, and black line through red eyes. Bluish-gray legs and feet. Long bill is hooked at tip.

Distribution Widespread throughout most of North America except southwestern US. Migrates to central South America in winter.

Call Prolific singers both in types and numbers of songs sang daily. Sings robin-like phrases most of the day from high in the canopy where it is difficult to see.

Habitat Nests and forages in deciduous and mixed pine-hardwood forests with heavy canopies. During migration, found in city parks with mature trees.

Feeding Hops on ground or along tree branches gleaning insects (caterpillars, spiders, aphids, ants, moths) in summer. Hook on bill is helpful for pulling insects out of crevices. Eats primarily fruit and berries in winter.

Nesting Female constructs an open-cup nest on forked branch using plant materials bound together by spider web silk. Exterior is camouflaged with lichens. Breed May–July; produce 1 brood of 3–5 eggs; incubate 11–15 days; fledge at 10–12 days.

Plants In winter, eats blackberries, elderberries, bayberries, and dogwood berries.

Water Drinks and bathes in water that has collected on or is dripping from leaves.

KINGLETS FAMILY
GOLDEN-CROWNED KINGLET
Regulus satrapa

Size 3¼–4¼ in (8–11 cm) long; 5½–7 in (14–18 cm) wingspan; ⅕ oz (6 g).

ID features Tiny, energetic birds that frequently flick their wings as they move quickly about. Olive-gray back, dull white belly, with black and white striped face and yellow crown. Males are distinguished by a bright orange patch in middle of crown. Short, notched tail; white wing bars; black legs and yellow feet; and thin black bill that is used for picking off tiny insects.

Distribution Found across much of Canada and northeastern and western regions of US. Northernmost birds winter in continental US.

Call A high, thin "seet" note uttered three at a time. Sings while foraging.

Habitat Breeds in the canopies of spruce, fir, and hemlock forests and uses a variety of woodland habitats in winter or during migration. Often found together with flocks of warblers and chickadees.

Feeding Eats mostly small insects. Hops along branches or hangs upside down on tips of branches gleaning spiders, spider eggs, mites, aphids, small beetles.

Nesting Both adults build a hammock-like nest suspended beneath thick protective needles on a conifer branch. Breed May–August; produce 1–2 broods of 8–9 eggs; incubate 14–15 days; fledge at 16–19 days.

Plants Nests lined with bark pieces, moss, lichens, and spiderweb silk.

Water Drinks from sap wells, birdbaths, or other natural water sources.

WOOD WARBLERS FAMILY
YELLOW-RUMPED WARBLER
Setophaga coronata

Size 5–6 in (13–15 cm) long; 7½–9 in (19–23 cm) wingspan; ½ oz (14 g).

ID features Called "Butterbutts" for their distinctive yellow rumps. Includes 2 subspecies: myrtle (eastern range), Audubon's (western range). In general, adult male myrtle warblers show black and white markings overall, white throat, black mask, and yellow flank patches. Audubon males have yellow throats, yellow side patches, and unmarked blue-gray heads. Females of each are duller in color. Dark legs and feet. Bill is thin and sharp.

Distribution Very common across North America. Winters in much of central and southeastern US, depending on weather and food availability in breeding range.

Call Calls and songs for each form vary. Myrtle call note a husky "tchik;" Audubon's a higher-pitched "jip."

Habitat Prefers open coniferous and mixed coniferous-hardwood forests. Winters in a variety of woodland habitats.

Feeding Mostly insects (caterpillars, aphids, flies, beetles, wasps) in summer from tree branches or flying out from a perch. In winter, feeds on berries, seeds.

Nesting Female prepares cup-shaped nest on horizontal branch consisting of twigs, pine needles, grasses lined with moss and fur. Breed March–August; produce 1–2 broods of 4–5 eggs; incubate 12–13 days; fledge at 12–14 days.

Plants "Myrtle" warbler gets its name from its ability to digest wax found in berries of wax myrtle and bayberry plants.

Water Will drink and bathe in shallow ponds, natural springs, or birdbaths.

AMERICAN REDSTART
Setophaga ruticilla

Size 4½–5½ in (11–14 cm) long; 7½–8 in (19–20 cm) wingspan; ¼ oz (7 g).

ID features Adult males are black and orange with a white belly. Females are olive-brown, have a white belly, and show yellow patches instead. It has black legs, feet, and bill. Its short bill is flat and surrounded by bristles that assist with detecting insects.

Distribution Breeds in southern Canada and across northern and eastern US. Migrates in winter to Central America and northern South America.

Call A harsh chip call; its short song is a rapid, high-pitched series of "see" notes.

Habitat Breeds in open woodlands near water but found during migration in wide range of habitats including shrubby areas.

Feeding Energetic and acrobatic forager of insects (moths, caterpillars, flies, spiders) from canopy twigs and leaves. Often flashes its wings or tail feathers to flush insects, which it then pursues.

Nesting Female constructs a tightly woven cup-shaped nest low in a dense shrub or fork of a tree using bark strips, grasses, pine needles, moss, and fur. Breed May–July; produce 1 brood of 2–5 eggs; incubate 10–13 days; fledge at 7–13 days.

Plants Prefers nesting in maple, birch, or ash trees or willow and alder thickets.

Water Obtains dietary water from juicy insects or drinks from dew drops, shallow puddles, or birdbaths.

YELLOW WARBLER
Setophaga petechia

Size 4½–5 in (11–13 cm) long; 6–9 in (16–22 cm) wingspan; ½ oz (14 g).

ID features Adult males have bright yellow coloration overall, unmarked faces with beady black eyes, rusty streaks on breast, and yellow-green backs and wings. Females are duller; underparts lack streaks. Legs and feet are pale brown; bills are short, stout, and sharp for gleaning insects from leaves.

Distribution Widespread throughout Alaska, Canada, and US, except the southwest and Gulf Coast regions. Migrates to southern US, Mexico, and Central and South America.

Call Usually sings from perches near tops of shrubs or small trees. Common breeding song is said to sound like, "sweet-sweet-I'm-so-sweet."

Habitat Prefers wet, brushy woodlands that include alder or willow thickets. Also found in orchards, suburban parks, or gardens.

Feeding Hops among branches gleaning insects (caterpillars, beetles, wasps, moths) and insect larvae.

Nesting Nest consists of a deep cup of plant material placed in a vertical fork of a tree or shrub. Monogamous pairs breed May–July; produce 1 brood of 4–5 eggs; incubate 11–14 days; fledge at 10–11 days.

Plants Nest materials include bark strips, grasses, plant fiber, and plant down.

Water Readily drinks and bathes from freshwater springs, fountains, or man-made water sources.

WOOD WARBLERS FAMILY
BLACK-AND-WHITE WARBLER
Mniotilta varia

Size 4⅓–5 in (11–13 cm) long; 7–9 in (18–22 cm) wingspan; ½ oz (14 g).

ID features Adult male features black and white streaked plumage lengthwise on body, with black ear patches, and two white wing bars. Females and juveniles show similar pattern but are duller and have less streaking. Short legs and long back toe, like nuthatches and creepers. Long, slightly curved bills for probing bark crevices for insects.

Distribution Widespread east of the Rocky Mountains in Canada and the US. Long distance migrant to southern US, Mexico, Central and South America.

Call Call is a sharp "stik." Song, a high-pitched "wheesy-wheesy wheezy," is said to sound like a squeaky wheel.

Habitat Prefers large deciduous trees in moist environments. Migrants are found in various habitats including city gardens and parks with mature trees and shrubs.

Feeding Moves nuthatch-like up and down tree trunks and along branches using its short legs and long back toe for support. Eats spiders, moth and butterfly larvae, ants, and beetles.

Nesting Female builds a cup nest on the ground in damp areas. Produce 1 brood of 4–6 eggs; incubate 10–12 days; fledge at 8–12 days.

Plants Uses bark, pine needles, dry leaves for nest, which is lined with moss and hair.

Water Perches in rain to bathe and drink droplets. Also uses streams or man-made water features.

CARDINALS FAMILY
NORTHERN CARDINAL
Cardinalis cardinalis

Size 8–9 in (21–23 cm) long; 10–12 in (25–30 cm) wingspan; 1½ oz (43 g).

ID features Known as the "Redbird," the male sports brilliant red plumage overall, with a black face and throat, a long tail, and a heavy red bill. The female has a red-orange bill and is reddish olive overall. Both have pointed crests and brown-gray legs and feet. Juveniles look like females but have dark colored bills.

Distribution Year-round resident of eastern and central North America from southern Canada to Mexico and Central America.

Call Call a sharp, hard "tik." Sings a robust "cheer-cheer-cheer" from some high perch. Unlike most songbirds, the female also sings, often while on her nest.

Habitat Found in dense thickets and shrubbery, forest edges, backyards. Frequent visitor to feeders.

Feeding Forages on the ground for insects (beetles, caterpillars, crickets) in summer; also provides these to nestlings. In winter, largely feeds on seeds and berries using its heavy bill to crush the hulls.

Nesting Nests are loose cups of twigs, grass, plant fiber, lined with pine needles, grass, and fur. Monogamous pair breeds April–September; produce 1–2 broods of 2–4 eggs; incubate 12–14 days; fledge at 9–12 days.

Plants Eats dogwood berries, blackberries, mulberries, and black oil sunflower seeds in feeders.

Water Drinks and bathes from ponds, streams, or birdbaths.

CARDINALS FAMILY
SCARLET TANAGER
Piranga olivacea

Size 6⅓–7 in (16–18 cm) long; 10–11½ in (25–29 cm) wingspan; 1 oz (28 g).

ID features Breeding male is bright scarlet-red on body and head with black wings and tail. Female has olive upperparts, yellowish underparts, and darker wings and tail. Non-breeding males look similar, but have black wings and tail. Legs and feet are dark gray. Bill is stout and pointed.

Distribution Found in lower eastern half of Canada and eastern half of US. Winters in northern and western South America.

Call Songs sound robin-like, though raspier like a "robin with a cold." Often heard while obscured from view in the high canopy.

Habitat Shy. Prefers canopies in deciduous woodlands, especially stands of mature oak trees.

Feeding Walks along branches high in the canopy searching for insects and larvae. May fly out to capture an insect. Will kill larger insects by pressing them into a branch before eating them. Will also eat fruits and berries in late summer/fall.

Nesting Female builds a loosely woven cup of twigs, grass, and fine material high up in the canopy. Breed May–July; produce 1 brood of 3–5 eggs; incubate 11–14 days; fledge at 9–11 days.

Plants Readily eats raspberries, strawberries, blackberries, serviceberries, and mulberries.

Water Drinks and bathes from shallow stream edges, puddles, or birdbaths.

CARDINALS FAMILY
ROSE-BREASTED GROSBEAK
Pheucticus ludovicianus

Size 7–8 in (18–20 cm) long; 11–13 in (28–33 cm) wingspan; 1½ oz (42 g).

ID features Breeding males have a striking rose-red breast, white belly, black head and back, black wings with white patches, and light-colored bill. Females look like large sparrow with large bill and distinctive white eyebrow stripe. Gray legs and toes are specialized for perching on branches and feeders. Its massive bill (from which it derives its name) crushes large seeds and hard-bodied insects.

Distribution Breeds in deciduous and mixed woodlands, orchards, and parks northeastern US and across Canada from Newfoundland to southeast Yukon. Migrates south in winter to Central and South America and the Caribbean.

Call Flutelike song similar to the American robin. Call note is a single sharp "kick" sound. Often first heard in thick canopies before spotted.

Habitat Woods, thickets, orchards, or feeders.

Feeding Eats insects, fruit, tree buds, and seeds.

Nesting Males and females work together to build loose, open cup nests in saplings. Parents share incubating, brooding, feeding. Breed May–July; produce 1–2 broods of 2–5 eggs, incubate 11–14 days; fledge at 9–12 days.

Plants Nests use twigs, leaves, and grass, lined by fur.

Water Drinks and bathes in streams, ponds, birdbaths.

BLACK-CAPPED CHICKADEE
Poecile atricapillus

Size 4–6 in (10–15 cm) long; 6–8 in (15–20 cm) wingspan; ⅜ oz (11 g).

ID features Sexes look alike. Black cap and throat, white cheeks, gray back and tail, whitish belly, and buffy flanks. Strong legs and feet enable quick, acrobatic moves while feeding. Small, short beak for cracking open seeds.

Distribution Nonmigratory. Resident of most of northern United States, Alaska, and southern Canada. Often seen in mixed flocks.

Call Song a loud, crisp whistle, "fee-bee" or "fee-bee-ee," with the first note higher. Alarm call mimics its name, "chick-a-dee-dee-dee."

Habitat Deciduous and mixed forests, urban and suburban parks.

Feeding Insects, insect eggs, and larvae in summer; seeds, berries, and suet in winter. Visits backyard bird feeders. Loves black oil sunflower seeds and hearts. Lowers body temperature to reduce energy loss.

Nesting Nests in woodpecker holes or natural cavities in birch and alder, or in nest boxes lined with wood shavings. Females build nests and line with moss, plant material, feathers, or fur. Breed April–June; produce 1 brood of 6–8 eggs; incubate 11–14 days; fledge at 14–18 days.

Plants Looks for seeds on wild plants and feeders.

Water Drinks from streams or birdbaths, or by eating snow.

MOUNTAIN CHICKADEE
Poecile gambeli

Size 5–6 in (13–15 cm) long; 7½–8½ in (19–22 cm) wingspan; ⅜ oz (11 g).

ID features Similar in coloration to black-capped chickadees but have unique white line above eyes. Strong feet support hanging upside down on pinecones. Bills slightly longer for probing hard-to-reach insects and larvae.

Distribution Year-round in coniferous forests in mountainous regions of western US and Canada. Often seen with nuthatches and kinglets.

Call Song is a 3- or 4-note descending whistle, "fee-bee-fee-bee," with the first note higher in pitch. Call a throaty "chick-a-dee-dee-dee" when alarmed.

Habitat Dry coniferous forests except during nesting season when they locate groves of aspen trees for their soft wood to excavate nests in.

Feeding Flits from outer twigs and branches looking for food. Eats caterpillars, spiders, insect eggs in summer; conifer seeds and berries in winter. Visits backyard feeders and readily takes black oil sunflower seeds and hearts as well as suet. Hides seeds for winter.

Nesting Cavity nesters; use old woodpecker holes or natural cavities; nest boxes. Females build nests and line with moss, lichens, grass, and fur. Breed April–July; produce 1–2 broods of 5–8 eggs; incubate 12–15 days; fledge at 18–21 days.

Plants Pine seeds, poison ivy berries, serviceberries, blueberries, walnuts, ragweed, sunflowers.

Water Drinks and bathes in shallow pools and streams or birdbaths.

NUTHATCHES FAMILY
WHITE-BREASTED NUTHATCH
Sitta carolinensis

Size 5–5¾ in (13–14 cm) long; 8–11 in (20–27 cm) wingspan; ¾ oz (21 g).

ID features Sexes similar. Blue-gray upperparts, white face and underparts with chestnut undertail, black crown and nape, short tail. Strong legs, feet, and claws which it uses to make jerky hops head-first up and down tree trunks and branches. Long, pointed bill.

Distribution Widespread across most of the US and southern Canada. Nonmigratory.

Call Most vocal during early spring and winter using different calls or songs to defend territory or for other purposes.

Habitat Found in mature and mixed deciduous woods, parks, orchards. Often visits feeders.

Feeding Forages along tree trunks and large branches to glean insects and larvae. Feeds on acorns and hickory nuts by pushing them into bark crevices and hammering out their contents with its sharp bill (derives its name from this activity). Readily eats black oil sunflower seeds, peanuts, and suet from feeders in winter, often caching food in bark of trees for later.

Nesting Uses abandoned woodpecker cavities or natural holes for nests, which are lined with fine grasses and fur. Breed April–July; produce 1 brood of 5–9 eggs; incubate 13–14 days; fledge at 18–26 days.

Plants Prefers mature hardwoods, especially oaks, for both nesting habitat and sources of insects and nuts.

Water Drinks and bathes in natural water sources or man-made water features.

CHICKADEES AND TITMICE FAMILY
TUFTED TITMOUSE
Baeolophus bicolor

Size 4½–5½ in (15–17 cm) long; 9–11 in (23–28 cm) wingspan; ¾ oz (21 g).

ID features Sexes look alike. Pale gray on back and head, black forehead, white belly with peach coloration on flanks. Black eyes and a short, pointed crest. Uses its feet to hold a seed or acorn and pounds it open with its stout, round bill.

Distribution Common backyard bird whose range has expanded. Resident of mature deciduous woods in eastern half of US to southern Canada.

Call Spring song is a cheerful, distinctive whistle, "peter peter peter peter." Gives a high-pitched alarm call when predators appear.

Habitat Woodlands, especially moist woods in swamps and river basins, parks, suburban backyards.

Feeding Flits through branches in search of caterpillars, ants, beetles, insect eggs. In winter, feeds on sunflower seeds, beechnuts, acorns, small fruits, and berries. Hides food for winter retrieval.

Nesting Cavity nester. Can't excavate own nests so will use natural cavities, old woodpecker holes, or nest boxes. Breed March–May; produce 1–2 broods of 5–7 eggs, incubate 12–14 days; fledge at 17–18 days.

Plants Lines nests with leaves, grass, moss, and fur.

Water Uses shallow birdbaths or pools for drinking and bathing; eats snow in winter if water is not available.

NUTHATCHES FAMILY
RED-BREASTED NUTHATCH
Sitta canadensis

Size 4½–5 in (11–12 cm) long; 8–8½ in (20–22 cm) wingspan; ⅜ oz (10 g).

ID features Males show distinct black and white head pattern, blue-gray upperparts, chestnut underparts, and short tails. Females slightly duller. Feet have strong toes and sharp claws for hitching up and down tree trunks. Bills are pointed and sharp.

Distribution Breeds in coniferous or mixed hardwood forests across Canada, Alaska, and northeastern and western regions of the US. Irruptive migrants to southern US depending on food availability in breeding range.

Call A one-note tin horn sounding "yank yank" call.

Habitat Prefers mature evergreen forests of rough barked coniferous trees with dense canopies and an understory of saplings for protection and sources of food. Found in other wooded habitats in the winter, including feeders.

Feeding Forages head-first up and down tree trunks and large branches for insects and larvae. In winter, eats conifer seeds, and sunflower seeds, peanuts, suet from feeders; caches seed in bark crevices and breaks them open with their sharp bill.

Nesting Excavates nest cavity in a soft-wood tree, lining it with grass, bark strips, fur, feathers. Applies pine resin around entrance opening to discourage predators. Breed May–July; produce 1 brood of 5–7 eggs; incubate 12–13 days; fledge at 18–21 days.

Plants Visits rough barked trees, not smooth barked.

Water Attracted to running water (streams, fountains) where it will drink and bathe.

TREECREEPERS FAMILY
BROWN CREEPER
Certhia americana

Size 5–5¾ in (13–15 cm) long; 7–8 in (17–20 cm) wingspan; ⅓ oz (9 g).

ID features Small, slender bird having white underparts and mottled brown upperparts serving to camouflage it against tree trunks. Strong toes with sharp claws for gripping bark; long stiff tail for support to creep up tree; a "moving piece of bark." Slightly downcurved bill.

Distribution Breeds widely across North America. Northernmost birds may migrate in winter to southern portion of breeding range.

Call Song a high-pitched "tsee tsee" followed by short trills, sung most of the day with variations.

Habitat Prefers mature and moist coniferous or mixed hardwood forests that contain stands of dead or dying trees for nesting and foraging.

Feeding Foraging habit is to start at base of a tree, hitch up trunk in a spiral fashion to top of tree, then fly to base of a nearby tree to repeat the process. Probes deep crevices with long bill for insects, eggs, larvae.

Nesting Forms unique hammock-like nest of twigs, moss, pine needles, and spider web silk beneath out-turned pieces of bark. Breed May–July; produce 1 brood of 5–6 eggs; incubate 14–17 days; fledge at 15–17 days.

Plants Favors ponderosa pine, spruce, eastern hemlock, and redwood trees for nesting, foraging.

Water Drinks and bathes in shallow streams and pools or man-made water features.

NORTHERN MOCKINGBIRD
Mimus polyglottos

Size 8½–10 in (22–25 cm) long; 13–15 in (33–38 cm) wingspan; 1¾ oz (52 g).

ID features Sexes alike. Gray head and upperparts, lighter underparts; dark gray wings; two white wing bars and large, white wing patches, which are frequently "flashed" in displays. Thin, black eye line. Long tail, black legs, feet, and slightly curved bill.

Distribution Year-round resident of most of the continental US and southern Canada.

Call Name means "many-tongued mimic." A prolific and incessant singer mimicking songs and sounds of other birds as well as non-bird noises. Uses a high perch to utter repetitive phrases.

Habitat Adapted to open environments with little vegetation; urban and suburban yards, parks, where grass is mowed.

Feeding Forages on the ground or in vegetation for insects during breeding season. May flash wings to scare insects out of hiding. Feeds on fruit and berries in fall and winter.

Nesting Monogamous pair builds its nest of twigs, lined with leaves, moss, and grass, inside a shrub or tree. Breed March–August; produce 2–4 broods of 3–5 eggs; incubate 11–14 days; fledge at 10–15 days.

Plants Favorite fruits include mulberries, raspberries, grapes, and dogwood berries.

Water Drinks and bathes from lake or river edges, puddles, or from water collected on plants.

GRAY CATBIRD
Dumetella carolinensis

Size 8–9½ in (20–24 cm) long; 10–12 in (25–30 cm) wingspan; 1⅓ oz (37 g).

ID features Sexes alike. Slate gray overall, black cap, and rust-colored undertail feathers. Large black eyes, blackish legs and feet, and straight black bill which it uses to flip over leaves in search of insects.

Distribution Widespread across southern Canada and in the US east of a diagonal line from Washington state to New Mexico. Winters along the Gulf Coast from Texas to Florida and into Central America.

Call Its catlike mewing call reflects its name. Mimics the songs of many birds repeating phrases only once. Often sings while hidden in a dense shrub.

Habitat Prefers dense brushy thickets or thorny tangles near water. Its name means "bird of the thorn bush." Found also in overgrown orchards, fencerows, farmlands, urban and suburban yards.

Feeding Opportunistic feeder. Eats a variety of insects and berries, whichever is most abundant. Forages on the ground or in low shrubs.

Nesting A bulky nest of twigs and bark, lined with grass, rootlets, or hair is built near the center of dense shrubbery. Breed May–August; produce 1–2 broods of 3–5 eggs; incubate 12–14 days; fledge at 8–12 days.

Plants Twigs, bark, and grass used for nest building.

Water Readily drinks and bathes from a birdbath or fountain drip. Attracted to running water.

CROWS AND JAYS FAMILY
STELLER'S JAY
Cyanocitta stelleri

Size 12–13 in (30–34 cm) long; 18–19 in (45–48 cm) wingspan; 4 oz (120 g).

ID features Sexes alike. Head, throat, upper back is charcoal gray; belly, wings, and tail are deep blue. Prominent, pointed crest. Black legs, feet, and long bill.

Distribution Western North America from Alaska, western provinces of Canada, western third of the US, into Mexico. Nonmigratory.

Call Call a scolding "Shaack! Shaack!" Mimics songs and sounds of many birds, squirrels, dogs, and mechanical devices.

Habitat Evergreen and mixed forests, farmland, and residential areas. Frequents backyard feeders.

Feeding Makes long hops on ground or in trees, foraging for insects or small vertebrates. Major part of diet is plant-based, especially acorns and pine seeds, which it hammers open with its stout bill. Frequent scavenger at picnic and campsites or visitor to backyard feeders for sunflower seeds, peanuts, or corn. Often caches food in ground or in trees for later.

Nesting Nests of twigs, pine needles, plant fibers cemented together with mud are built on horizontal branch of conifer tree near trunk. Breed March–July; produce 1 brood of 3–5 eggs; incubate 16–18 days; fledge at 18–21 days.

Plants Uses twigs and pine needles for nesting.

Water Drinks and bathes in shallow creeks, fountains, or birdbaths.

CROWS AND JAYS FAMILY
BLUE JAY
Cyanocitta cristata

Size 9½–12 in (24–30 cm) long; 13–17 in (34–43 cm) wingspan; 3 oz (85 g).

ID features Sexes alike. Bright blue and white on wings and tail; blue crest and back; white face, throat, and underparts. Long tail. Black necklace, legs and feet, and bill. Noisy, but highly curious and intelligent birds.

Distribution Widespread across southern Canada east of the Rocky Mountains, eastern and central US. Largely nonmigratory.

Call Call a familiar harsh scream, "Jay! Jay!" Frequently mimics calls of several hawks.

Habitat Breeds in coniferous and deciduous forests, especially those containing oak trees. Also found in urban and suburban areas, backyard feeders.

Feeding Forages on the ground and in trees for insects, though primarily eats acorns and seeds. Holds acorns or large seeds with feet and cracks them open with strong bill. Often caches them in the ground for later. Also eats peanuts, cracked corn, and black oil sunflower seeds from feeders. Associates in small flocks.

Nesting Monogamous pair builds cup-shaped nest of twigs containing bark strips, moss, rootlets, feathers, paper, cemented together with some mud. Breed March–July; produce 1 brood of 4–5 eggs; incubate 16–18 days; fledge at 18–20 days.

Plants Builds nest on horizontal branch in coniferous or deciduous trees or dense shrubs.

Water Readily drinks and bathes from shallow ponds or birdbaths.

CROWS AND JAYS FAMILY
AMERICAN CROW
Corvus brachyrhynchos

Size 16–20 in (40–5 cm) long; 35–40 in (89–102 cm) wingspan; 16 oz (450 g).

ID features Sexes alike. Large, chunky bird that is black overall, including its bill, legs, and feet. Tail is short and squared; legs and feet are long and strong; bill is straight and heavy. Inquisitive, intelligent, and resourceful birds.

Distribution Common across most of Canada and US, except desert southwest.

Call Familiar, loud "caaw-caaw-caaw." Known to mimic sounds of other birds and animals. Often seen noisily mobbing predators and threats.

Habitat Adapted to almost all open habitats; farmland, city parks, roadsides, landfills. Highly social and organizes in winter into large flocks to roost.

Feeding An opportunist that eats nearly anything. Forages on ground for insects, fruit, berries, nuts, garbage, carrion. Also eats other birds' eggs and chicks from nests.

Nesting Monogamous pair; offspring from previous year may help parents feed nestlings. Build cup nest of sticks, lined with soft bark, pine needles, and fur, near tree trunk. Breed April–June; produce 1 brood of 4–6 eggs; incubate 16–18 days; fledge at 28–35 days.

Plants Sticks, bark, and pine needles for nesting.

Water Bathes and drinks from stream edges, shallow ponds, or birdbaths. Known to "dip" food to provide water to nestlings.

CROWS AND JAYS FAMILY
BLACK-BILLED MAGPIE
Pica hudsonia

Size 18–24 in (45–60 cm) long; 22–24 in (56–61 cm) wingspan; 6½ oz (192 g).

ID features Sexes alike. Head, back, upper breast a rich black contrasted with bright white belly and shoulders. Feathers of wings and tail show iridescent blue-green. White wing patches flash in-flight; long tail enables it to make rapid changes in direction. Tail accounts for about half its length. Legs, feet, and bill are black.

Distribution Range extends from southern coastline of Alaska to western half of Canada and US south to northern edges of Arizona, New Mexico, and Texas.

Call Utters a noisy "mag-mag-mag" call.

Habitat Prefers open habitats near water and thickets for protection. Found in farmlands, meadows, towns, and suburban areas. Frequently singing while perched in tops of trees, on road signs, or on fence posts.

Feeding Opportunistic omnivore. Eats nearly anything while foraging on the ground. Uses its bill or feet to uncover insects. Eats primarily animal matter (insects, worms, eggs, carrion), but also berries and seeds. Uses sense of smell to locate food. Commonly caches food in the ground using its bill.

Nesting Nests are large (30 in high, 20 in wide), formed like a dome. Monogamous pair breeds March–June; produce 1 brood of 5–8 eggs; incubate 16–21 days; fledge at 24–30 days.

Plants Uses twigs, rootlets, grass, pine needles, and mud in nests.

Water Nearby water sources used for bathing and drinking.

BALTIMORE ORIOLE
Icterus galbula

Size 8–10 in (20–26 cm) long; 10–12 in (26–30 cm) wingspan; 1⅕ oz (33 g).

ID features Males have solid black heads, upper breast, and tails with bright orange underparts, shoulder patches, and rump. Females have dull orange-yellow head, back, and underparts; gray-brown wings with two white wing bars. Both sexes have long legs and feet that are blackish-gray. Bill is straight, pointed, and black.

Distribution Range is eastern and east-central North America. Winters in Central and South America.

Call A clear melodious 1–2 note flutelike song that is heard from the high canopies of deciduous trees.

Habitat Found in open deciduous woods near rivers or streams or among shade trees in suburban areas.

Feeding Gleans insects from leafy canopies, especially caterpillars and spiders. Also eats ripe, dark-colored fruits (mulberries, cherries, grapes). Frequent visitor at feeders for sliced oranges, grape jelly, and nectar.

Nesting Monogamous pair builds a socklike nest of tightly woven grass and plant materials hung from the underside of a branch toward its end. Breed May–July; produce 1 brood of 4–5 eggs; incubate 12–14 days; fledge at 12–14 days.

Plants Nests are built in elm trees, maples, willows, and cottonwoods.

Water Drinks and bathes in birdbaths and is attracted to sound of moving water.

COMMON GRACKLE
Quiscalus quiscula

Size 11–13½ in (28–34 cm) long; 15–18 in (38–46 cm) wingspan; 4 oz (115 g).

ID features Males show glossy black plumage with bronze, purple, or green iridescence on back depending on forms. Dark head and wings, pale yellow eyes. Females are duller overall and slightly smaller. Long, V-shaped tails; long legs and feet; stout, straight black bill.

Distribution Common and widespread across North America east of the Rocky Mountains. Year-round resident in most of its range, though northern birds migrate to the southeastern US. Very social; form large flocks in winter to roost and forage.

Call Call is a deep, harsh "chek." Song mechanical or squeaky. Mimics other birds, though not expertly.

Habitat Well adapted to human environments. Found in open woodlands, marshes, cropland, city parks, residential areas.

Feeding Omnivorous. Forages on the ground for beetles, crickets, spiders, flies, worms, minnows in streams, and small vertebrates. Eats corn, rice, seeds, and berries. Steals food from other birds.

Nesting Bulky nest of twigs, grass, leaves, and fur reinforced by mud is concealed in dense conifer tree or shrub. Breed April–July; produce 1 brood of 5–6 eggs; incubate 12–14 days; fledge at 12–15 days.

Plants Twigs and leaves to build nest in conifers.

Water Drinks and bathes from shallow streams or birdbaths. Known to "dunk" food in water before eating.

NEW WORLD SPARROWS FAMILY
DARK-EYED JUNCO
Junco hyemalis

Size 5–6½ in (12½–16½ cm) long; 8–10 in (20–26 cm) wingspan; ⅔ oz (20 g).

ID features Multiple subspecies exist with much variation in back and head coloration. Most have gray or brown head and breast with white belly. Colors and markings are darker, more distinct in males than females. Juncos are distinguished by their outer white tail feathers, conspicuous in-flight, and small pale (pinkish) legs, feet, and conical bills.

Distribution Widespread throughout Canada and US. Known as the "snowbirds," most winter from southern Canada into Mexico.

Call Call a crisp "tick!" Male sings a fluid one-note, high-pitched trill.

Habitat Breeds in coniferous or deciduous forests. Found other times in open wooded areas with dense ground cover; roadsides, parks, gardens, backyards.

Feeding About 75 percent of diet from grass or weed seeds; during summer pecks and scratches ground for insects. Visits winter feeders for sunflower seeds and millet.

Nesting Nest built on the ground beneath a grassy overhang, exposed tree roots, or rock ledge. Breed May–August; produce 1–2 broods of 3–5 eggs; incubate 12–13 days; fledge at 10–13 days.

Plants Female weaves together small twigs, leaves, moss around her body and lines cup with fine grass, hair, or feathers.

Water Eats snow during winter; otherwise, drinks and bathes in streams, pools, or water collected on plants.

NEW WORLD SPARROWS FAMILY
AMERICAN TREE SPARROW
Spizella arborea

Size 5½–6½ in (14–16½ cm) long; 8½–10 in (22–25 cm) wingspan; ¾ oz (22 g).

ID features Sexes alike. Adults show a rusty cap, gray face with black eye line, rusty streaked back, brown wings with two white wing bars, light underparts with black spot on breast. Dark legs and feet. Short, bicolored black and yellow bill.

Distribution Breeds near or above the treeline from Alaska across northern Canada. Winters across southern Canada and northern two-thirds of US.

Call Male sings a single bell-like song to defend his territory.

Habitat Breeds in boggy habitats of tundra with scrubby thickets; scattered small trees used by males to sing in. Migrates in winter, found in variety of habitats including open fields, brushy roadsides, marshes, suburban areas; forms large flocks to forage.

Feeding Forages on the ground or low bushes in search of insects (summer); weed and grass seeds, berries in winter. In winter often beats its wings to dislodge seeds from grass heads.

Nesting Nest cup usually built on ground concealed by dense shrubbery. Female uses grasses, bark pieces, moss, and lines it with feathers, fine grasses. Breed May–August; produce 1 brood of 4–6 eggs; incubate 12–13 days; fledge at 8–10 days.

Plants Eats seeds of grasses, ragweed, goldenrod, sedges.

Water Drinks about 30 percent of its weight daily. Bathes frequently; eats snow in winter.

SONG SPARROW
Melospiza melodia

Size 5–7 in (13–18 cm) long; 8½–10 in (22–25 cm) wingspan; ¾ oz (22 g).

ID features Sexes alike. Brown cap and eye line, gray cheeks, and streaked back. Long, brown rounded tail; white breast with brown coarse streaks and a central dark spot. Pinkish legs and feet; dusky gray bill.

Distribution Common and widespread from Alaska across southern half of Canada to north-central and northeastern US. Northern range birds migrate in winter to southern US or Mexico.

Call Dry "tchip" call. Male perches on top of bush or small tree, tilts head back, and sings a series of trills and crisp notes before changing to a different song.

Habitat Found in a variety of open habitats: marshes, shelterbelts, roadsides, forest edges.

Feeding Walks or hops quietly on ground through grasses, weeds, and low shrubs. In summer, eats insects (beetles, grasshoppers, spiders, caterpillars). In fall and winter, feeds on seeds and berries.

Nesting Female builds cup-shaped nest on ground hidden in grasses or weeds near water. Built using weeds, bark, rootlets, and fur. Breed March–August; produce 1–3 broods of 3–5 eggs; incubate 12–14 days; fledge at 10–12 days.

Plants Eats buckwheat, sunflower seeds, wheat, rice, raspberries, blueberries, mulberries.

Water Frequents edges of lakes, marshes, or ground-level birdbaths to drink and bathe.

CHIPPING SPARROW
Spizella passerina

Size 5–6 in (13–15 cm) long; 8–9 in (20–23 cm) wingspan; ½ oz (15 g).

ID features Known locally as the "chippies." Sexes alike. Adult breeders show bright russet cap; distinctive white eyebrow and black eye line; gray cheeks, rump, and belly; brown wings with two white wing bars. Long notched tail. Legs and feet are deep pink; bill is conical, short, and blackish.

Distribution Found throughout North America. Northern populations migrate and winter in southern US and Mexico.

Call Call a hard "tsip" made throughout the day while foraging. Male sings a uniform, one-pitched trill from his perch atop a high branch.

Habitat Breeds in shrubby, grassy, or open woodland areas, but adapted to other habitats; open woods with shrubby undergrowth, farms, towns, seashores, orchards, city parks.

Feeding Forages on the ground for insects (caterpillars, moths, grasshoppers, crickets, beetles) in the summer and seeds of grass, weeds, or waste grain in fall and winter. Also visits feeders.

Nesting Female constructs a flimsy nest in a young conifer tree or shrub. Materials include platform of rootlets and grasses lined by fine plant fibers and fur. Breed April–July; produce 1–2 broods of 3–5 eggs; incubate 10–12 days; fledge at 9–12 days.

Plants Readily eats crabgrass, ragweed, dandelion, clover, and foxtail.

Water Drinks and bathes in shallow pools, streams, or birdbaths.

NEW WORLD SPARROWS FAMILY
WHITE-CROWNED SPARROW
Zonotrichia leucophrys

Size 6–7 in (15–18 cm) long; 9–10 in (22–25 cm) wingspan; 1 oz (28 g).

ID features Sexes alike. Breeding adults show bold black and white stripes on head; gray cheeks, throat, and belly; brown streaked back; brown wings with two white wing bars. Long tail. Pinkish legs, feet, and conical bill.

Distribution Breeds in open brushy or alpine meadow habitats of northernmost parts of North America. Northern populations are migratory to US and central Mexico.

Call Call a sharp "pink!" as an alarm call. Song a short set of sweet, clear whistles followed by a series of buzzy warbles.

Habitat Found in a variety of habitats in winter and migration, especially forest edges, thickets, roadsides, overgrown fields, city parks, backyards.

Feeding Hops on the ground or in low shrubs foraging for insects, seeds, buds, berries, and fruit. Insects mainly consumed in summer; plant matter in fall and winter.

Nesting Bulky cup nest is built by female on or near ground or in bushes. Consists of twigs, bark strips, moss, leaves lined by feathers, grass, and fur. Breed March–August; produce 1–3 broods of 4–5 eggs; incubate 11–14 days; fledge at 8–10 days.

Plants Eats seeds of grasses, weeds, corn, barley, willow catkins, elderberries, blackberries.

Water Drinks and bathes at shallow streams and birdbaths.

NEW WORLD SPARROWS FAMILY
WHITE-THROATED SPARROW
Zonotrichia albicollis

Size 6–7 in (15–18 cm) long; 9–10 in (23–26 cm) wingspan; 1 oz (28 g).

ID features Sexes alike. Bold head color pattern (black and white or black and tan crown stripes) depending on forms, black eye line, yellow spot between eye and bill, clear white throat, gray face and belly. Brown back with dark streaks, wings reddish-brown with two white wing bars. Pink legs and feet; small, grayish bill.

Distribution Breeds across Canada, north-central, and northeast US. Winters in south-central and eastern US.

Call Call a loud, sharp "jink!" Whistles a rhythmic song remembered by "Oh sweet Canada Canada Canada."

Habitat Breeds in northern pine and deciduous forests to treeline where there are openings of low, dense vegetation. In winter and migration found in fencerows, thickets, city parks, suburban backyards.

Feeding Hops and scratches leaf litter with both feet to uncover insects and seeds on ground. Mainly eats seeds, buds, fruit.

Nesting Nests built over depressions on the ground using pieces of moss, grasses, twigs, pine needles, lined with rootlets and animal hair. Concealed by leaves. Breed May–August; produce 1–2 broods of 4–5 eggs; incubate 11–14 days; fledge at 8–9 days.

Plants Eats ragweed, buckwheat, grapes, blueberries, sumac, dogwood, mountain ash.

Water Uses shallow surface water and ground level birdbaths to drink and bathe in.

FINCHES FAMILY
HOUSE FINCH
Haemorhous mexicanus

Size 5–6 in (12½–15 cm) long; 8–10 in (20–25 cm) wingspan; ¾ oz (22 g).

ID features Adult males have rosy red face, eyebrow, throat, upper breast, and rump. Back, belly, and long notched tail are streaked brown. Females are brown overall with streaked underparts. Gray-brown legs, feet, and conical seed-eating bill.

Distribution Widespread across southernmost Canada and throughout the US occupying a variety of habitats. Largely nonmigratory.

Call Call note sounds like "queet!" Male sings a cheery, rapid but disjointed warble atop a high perch.

Habitat Varies from its native dry, desert settings in the West to rural, urban, and suburban areas elsewhere; city parks, farms, forest edges, backyards, feeders. Gregarious, social.

Feeding Forages on the ground in low vegetation eating almost exclusively plant matter such as buds, fruits, seeds. Frequent visitor to feeders for black oil sunflower seeds, millet, or niger seed.

Nesting Female builds cup nest in trees or man-made structures using small twigs, grass stems, rootlets, feathers. Breed March–August; produce 1–3 broods of 4–5 eggs; incubate 12–14 days; fledge at 12–15 days.

Plants Unlike other birds, parents feed nestlings plant matter, especially dandelion seeds.

Water Uses available surface water, shallow streams, or birdbaths for drinking and bathing.

FINCHES FAMILY
AMERICAN GOLDFINCH
Spinus tristis

Size 4–5½ in (10–14 cm) long; 7½–9 in (19–23 cm) wingspan; ⅔ oz (20 g).

ID features Breeding males have lemon yellow bodies, white rumps, black forehead and wings with white markings, orange-ish bill. Females and non-breeding males are olive-brown overall with black wings and white markings. Undergoes seasonal molts of body feathers in late winter and late summer. Agile legs and feet well adapted for holding onto weed stem while removing seeds from plant head. Conical bill.

Distribution Common and widespread from southern regions of Canada and throughout the US. Migrates into southern parts of US in response to colder weather, food availability.

Call Produces "per-twee-twee-twee" call during flights between foraging sites. Song is light and canary-like.

Habitat Prefers open country with abundant weeds and annual grasses; roadsides, flood plains, fields and meadows, suburban gardens.

Feeding Almost exclusively seed eaters. Also, eats sunflower and niger seeds from feeders.

Nesting Female builds tightly woven nest in branches of a shrub or tree using bark, grass, weed stems, reinforced by spider web silk and lined with plant down. Breed late July–September; produce 1–2 broods of 4–6 eggs; incubate 12–14 days; fledge at 11–17 days.

Plants Feeds on thistle, goatsbeard, dandelions, coneflowers, birch catkins.

Water Drinks and bathes from rain puddles, birdbaths, natural water sources.

FINCHES FAMILY
PINE SISKIN
Spinus pinus

Size 4¼–5½ in (11–14 cm) long; 7–9 in (18–23 cm) wingspan; ½ oz (15 g).

ID features Brown upperparts, light brown underparts, heavily streaked throughout. Short, forked tail. Wings, tail tinged with yellow. Legs and feet are dark. Strong feet and toes enable birds to hang upside down on pinecones or seed heads while using sharply pointed forcepslike bill to pry out small seeds.

Distribution Widespread across North America. Breeding range in open coniferous and mixed forests extends from northern Canada and Alaska to western mountainous and northern regions of US. An irruptive winter finch that migrates in large flocks south in search of food.

Call Quite vocal. Flocks of birds heard before seen. Call a distinctive "zreeeee" made with wheezy voice.

Habitat Nomadic. Winter flocks found in open deciduous woods, parkland, roadsides, weedy meadows, suburban yards.

Feeding Forages in trees, shrubs, or weedy areas for seeds, plant stems, occasional insects. Frequent visitor to feeders for niger seed and sunflower chips.

Nesting Female builds a shallow cup of twigs, leaves, bark strips, grass lined with feathers, fur, thistle down. Breed February–August; produce 1–2 broods of 3–5 eggs; incubate 12–13 days; fledge at 13–17 days.

Plants Favors seeds of spruce, hemlock, tamarack, birch, alder, and maples.

Water Drinks and bathes from natural cavities, shallow surface water, and birdbaths.

FINCHES FAMILY
COMMON REDPOLL
Acanthis flammea

Size 4½–5½ in (11–14 cm) long; 8¼–9 in (21–23 cm) wingspan; ½ oz (15 g).

ID features Males have bright red patch on forehead, pinkish breast. Females lack pink breast, forehead patch smaller. Brown-gray finches darkly streaked on back and flanks, black chin, notched tail, two white wing bars, tiny yellow pointed bill.

Distribution Breeding range from Alaska across northernmost parts of Canada. Winters across the remainder of Canada into northern parts of US. Irruptive migrant; large flocks periodically seen in central to southern US searching for food.

Call Variety of calls given to maintain contact within flock. Song a series of trills, repeated notes.

Habitat Breeds in open stands of spruce, pine, willow, alder, birch. In winter, nomadic flocks descend on similar wooded stands or fields of weeds and brush to forage. Visits backyard feeders.

Feeding In summer, consumes spiders and insects. Throughout year feeds on seeds from birch, alder, willow, spruce; also, buds, grasses, sedges. Eats millet, niger seeds at feeders.

Nesting Female builds cup nest of twigs, grass, moss lined with feathers, fur, or plant down. Breed May–July; produce 1–2 broods of 4–6 eggs; incubate 10–13 days; fledge at 12–15 days.

Plants Diet relies heavily on birch and alder catkins.

Water Drinks and bathes in shallow streams, lake edges, birdbaths. Also eats snow in winter.

RED CROSSBILL
Loxia curvirostra

Size 5¼–6½ in (13–16 cm) long; 10–11 in (25–27 cm) wingspan; 1 oz (30 g).

ID features Males dull red or orange; females dull olive-yellow. Dark brown wings, no wing bars. Hangs from branch or cone by its strong feet. Bill tips crossed and specialized for extracting seeds from conifer cones.

Distribution Year-round residents of coniferous forests from southern coast of Alaska across Canada to western, mountainous, very north-central, and northeast regions of the US. Irruptive migrants; nomadic flocks may appear in parks or suburbs in other parts of the US.

Call A series of sharp "jip-jip-jip" notes repeated several times as they fly overhead.

Habitat Found in mature coniferous forests wherever there is a large cone crop.

Feeding Primarily seed eater, preferring seeds from pines, spruce, hemlock, fir, and larch. Also eats seeds of alder and birch, berries, and insects (aphids). Comes to roadsides for grit to aid digestion of seeds.

Nesting Female builds nest on horizontal branch in coniferous tree using twigs, grass, weeds, pine needles, feathers, hair. Can breed year-round if cone crop is good. Produce 1–2 broods of 3–5 eggs; incubate 12–16 days; fledge at 18–22 days.

Plants Does not wander far from conifer forests. Eats sunflower, niger seeds at feeders.

Water Drinks and bathes in springs, streams, or birdbaths. Also eats snow.

EVENING GROSBEAK
Coccothraustes vespertinus

Size 6½–9 in (17–23 cm) long; 12–14 in (30–36 cm) wingspan; 2 oz (60 g).

ID features Males show bright yellow forehead and eyebrow; dark grayish head, back, and throat; mustard yellow shoulders and belly. Females grayish overall with some yellow on nape. Both have black wings and tails with distinctive white wing patches; pink legs and feet; heavy, pale bills.

Distribution Residents of Rocky Mountains eastward across Canada into western mountainous regions of US and Mexico. Irruptive migrants; large flocks occasionally move into US in search of food.

Call Uses a series of trills, chatters, or flight calls to maintain contact within a flock.

Habitat Found year-round in coniferous and mixed forests. In winter, may also be found in rural or suburban woodlands and at feeders.

Feeding Forages in trees and shrubs for seeds, fruits, and insects (especially spruce budworm larvae, caterpillars, aphids). At feeders, consumes abundant amounts of sunflower seeds using its heavy bill to crush seeds.

Nesting Loose nest of twigs and rootlets lined with pine needles, lichens, or grasses built by female in tree or shrub. Breed May–July; produce 1–2 broods of 3–4 eggs; incubate 12–14 days; fledge at 13–14 days.

Plants Eats seeds of spruce, fir, pine, box elder, maple, ash, and fruits; crab apple, juniper berries, cherries.

Water Drinks and bathes in open stream edges, rain puddles, and birdbaths.

INDEX OF BIRDS BY COMMON NAME

INDEX

PICTURE CREDITS

The publisher would like to thank the following for their kind permission to reproduce their photographs:

(Key: a-above; b-below/bottom; c-center; f-far; l-left; r-right; t-top)

1 Dreamstime.com: Svetlana Foote (cb); Michael Truchon (ca). 3 Dreamstime.com: (cra, clb). 4 Dreamstime.com: Svetlana Foote (cb). 5 Alamy Stock Photo: DanitaDelimont.com / Richard & Susan Day (fbl, bl). Dreamstime.com: Charles Brutlag (tl); Steve Byland (tr). 8 123RF.com: rck953 (tl). Dreamstime.com: Charles Brutlag (cb). 9 Alamy Stock Photo: Rolf Nussbaumer Photography / Bill Draker (tr). 10 Alamy Stock Photo: Rolf Nussbaumer Photography. 12 Alamy Stock Photo: Reimar (cb). 13 Dreamstime.com: Petar Kremenarov (t). 14 Dorling Kindersley: Alan Murphy (cla). Dreamstime.com: Petar Kremenarov (cb). 15 Dreamstime.com: Michael Truchon / Mtruchon (clb). 16 Dreamstime.com: Paul Roedding (tr); Wei Kee Teoh (tr). 17 Alamy Stock Photo: Sharon Talson (cl). Dreamstime.com: Forestpath (tl). 18 Alamy Stock Photo: Oleh Honcharenko (cr). Dreamstime.com: Jessamine (bl/nest); NatmacStock (bl); Steven Smith (cr/dove). 19 Dreamstime.com: Melvin Ray Herr (cl); Thejipen (ftr); Bruce Macqueen (tr). 20 Dreamstime.com: Cheryl Davis (bl). 21 123RF.com: rck953 (cb). Dreamstime.com: Balázs Justin (tl). 22 Dreamstime.com: Randall Runtsch (bl). 23 Dreamstime.com: Charles Brutlag (cr); Wildphotos (tr); Paul Reeves (bc). 24 Dreamstime.com: Rinus Baak (b); Jgorzynik (tr). 25 Dreamstime.com: Sue Feldberg (cra); Mikelane45 (cb). 26 Dorling Kindersley: Alan Murphy (crb). Dreamstime.com: Benjaminboeckle (cl). 27 Dreamstime.com: Michael Truchon (br). naturepl.com: Alan Murphy / BIA (cra). 28 Dreamstime.com: Charles Brutlag (br); Vasiliy Vishnevskiy (cra). 29 Dreamstime.com: Steve Byland (br); Brian Kushner (tl). 30 Dreamstime.com: K Quinn Ferris (bl). 31 Dreamstime.com: Rinus Baak (br); George Jones (tr). 32 Alamy Stock Photo: Rolf Nussbaumer Photography / Bill Draker (tr). 33 Alamy Stock Photo: DanitaDelimont.com / Richard & Susan Day (clb, cb, crb). Dreamstime.com: Gerald Deboer (tr). 34 Dreamstime.com: Steve Byland (fcla); Bruce Macqueen (cra); Svetlana Foote (tl). 35 Dreamstime.com: Charles Brutlag (cb). 36 Dreamstime.com: John Fader. 38 naturepl.com: Alan Murphy (bl). 39 Dreamstime.com: Charles Brutlag (cl); Brian Lasenby (tl). naturepl.com: Doug Wechsler (crb). 40 Alamy Stock Photo: All Canada Photos / Nick Saunders (tr). Dreamstime.com: Brian Kushner (cra). 41 Alamy Stock Photo: All Canada Photos / Glenn Bartley (tr). Dreamstime.com: Lukas Blazek (cla); Ondřej Prosický (cra); Senorrojo (bl). 42 Dreamstime.com: Andrey Starostin (br). 43 Dreamstime.com: Oksana Ermak (tl). 45 Dreamstime.com: Mario Bonotto (tr); Bert Folsom (tl). 48 Alamy Stock Photo: Simon J Beer (crb). naturepl.com: David Tipling (clb). 49 Dreamstime.com: Moose Henderson (cr). wildlifeworld.co.uk: (cl). 50 Alamy Stock Photo: Daybreak Imagery (cl). Dreamstime.com: Stuart Monk (r). 51 Alamy Stock Photo: John Van Decker (tl). Dreamstime.com: Steveheap (tr). Getty Images: Universal Images Group / Education Images (br). 58 Alamy Stock Photo: Kristina Blokhin (cla). Dreamstime.com: Steve Byland (cra); Bruce Macqueen (cl); Svetlana Foote (c); Sarah Marchant (cb). 59 Dreamstime.com: Charles Brutlag (br); Andrew Vanhooser (t). Dreamstime.com: Photosbyjam (bl); Michael Truchon (t). © duncraft.com: (crb). 66 CJ Wildlife / Vivara: (cla). Dorling Kindersley: Robert Royse (tc). wildlifeworld.co.uk: (bc). 67 Dreamstime.com: Steve Byland (tr). 68 Alamy Stock Photo: William Leaman (b). 71 Alamy Stock Photo: FLPA. 72 CJ Wildlife / Vivara: (bc). 73 Dreamstime.com: Charles Brutlag (crb); Paul Reeves (cra). 74 CJ Wildlife / Vivara: (cl, cr). 75 Dreamstime.com: Mike Trewet (tr). wildlifeworld.co.uk: (cl). 76 Alamy Stock Photo: Panther Media GmbH / steffstarr (cl). Dreamstime.com: Melodyanne (cr). 77 Alamy Stock Photo: Paul Mogford (cl). Dreamstime.com: Jillian Cain (tl). FLPA: Chris & Tilde Stuart (bl). 78 wildlifeworld.co.uk: (br). 79 wildlifeworld.co.uk: (bl). 83 wildlifeworld.co.uk: (cl). 84 Alamy Stock Photo: Paul Mogford (cra). wildlifeworld.co.uk: (bl). 85 CJ Wildlife / Vivara: (cl, tl). Dreamstime.com: Petar Kremenarov (cr). 88 Alamy Stock Photo: Liam Bunce (bl). 92 Dreamstime.com: Miriam Doerr (bl). 93 Alamy Stock Photo: blickwinkel / Hecker (cl). 94 Dorling Kindersley: Alan Murphy (cla). Dreamstime.com: Steve Byland (crb). 96 Alamy Stock Photo: Doris Dumrauf. 98 Dreamstime.com: Leerobin (crb). 99 Dorling Kindersley: Robert Royse (cb). Dreamstime.com: Steve Byland (cra). 101 Dreamstime.com: Marekusz (tc). 104 Dorling Kindersley: Downderry Nursery (crb); RHS Wisley

(cr). Dreamstime.com: Dariaren (clb). 105 Dorling Kindersley: Neil Fletcher (tl); RHS Wisley (tr). 107 Dorling Kindersley: Tom Grey (cla/Blackbird); Natural History Museum, London (c, cla). Dreamstime.com: Péter Gudella (cb); Wildphotos (tl); Mikelane45 (tc); Brent Hathaway (cb). 108 Alamy Stock Photo: Bob Gibbons (cr). Dorling Kindersley: Mark Winwood / RHS Wisley (cl). 109 Dorling Kindersley: Mark Winwood / RHS Wisley (bl). Dreamstime.com: Michael Vi (tr). 110 Alamy Stock Photo: Nature Photographers Ltd / Brian E Small (cra). Dreamstime.com: Charles Brutlag (fcra). 111 Dreamstime.com: Petar Kremenarov (cb). 112 123RF.com: Leonid Ikan (crb); timyee (cr). Dreamstime.com: Yuliya Borodina (cl). 114 Alamy Stock Photo: FLPA (clb). 116 Dreamstime.com: Jeans550 (cr); Calvin L. Leake (crb). 117 Depositphotos Inc: swimwitdafishes (cb). Dreamstime.com: Poravute Siriphiroon (cr). 120 Alamy Stock Photo: DanitaDelimont.com / Richard & Susan Day (clb, cb). Dreamstime.com: Mikelane45 (tc). 121 Dreamstime.com: Svetlana Foote (cra). 122 Alamy Stock Photo: Danita Delimont / Rolf Nussbaumer. 124 Dreamstime.com: Mikelane45 (cra). 125 Dreamstime.com: Charles Brutlag (cb); Svetlana Foote (clb). 126 Shutterstock.com: Hayley Crews (cb). 127 Alamy Stock Photo: BC Photo (tr). 133 Dorling Kindersley: Forrest L. Mitchell / James Laswel (cla). Dreamstime.com: Rck953 (ca); Rudmer Zwerver / Creativenature1 (cb). 139 Alamy Stock Photo: Arterra Picture Library / Arndt Sven-Erik (tr); Janice and Nolan Braud (crb). Dreamstime.com: Roman Ivaschenko (tl). wildlifeworld.co.uk: (cr). 140 Alamy Stock Photo: DP Wildlife Invertebrates (clb). Dorling Kindersley: Jerry Young (cr). naturepl.com: Tom Walmsley (crb). 141 Dreamstime.com: Rostislav Stefanek (cl). 143 Alamy Stock Photo: Mike Ford (tl). 144 Alamy Stock Photo: Eye vision (ca). CJ Wildlife / Vivara: (bc/Cage). Dorling Kindersley: Robert Royse (cb, bc/Carolina Chickadee). Dreamstime.com: Charles Brutlag (cra). 145 CJ Wildlife / Vivara: (cra/Cage). Dreamstime.com: Charles Brutlag (ca/Junco, cra/Junco); Petar Kremenarov (cra). 146 Alamy Stock Photo: All Canada Photos / Stephen Krasemann. 148 CJ Wildlife / Vivara: (cr, crb/Cage). Dorling Kindersley: Robert Royse (cra). Dreamstime.com: Charles Brutlag (crb/used 4 times). 149 Alamy Stock Photo: Eye vision (tc). 150 Dreamstime.com: Ian Mcglasham (bl). 151 Alamy Stock Photo: David Bratley (t). 152 Alamy Stock Photo: Gillian Pullinger (bl). 153 Alamy Stock Photo: Rick & Nora Bowers (bl). Shutterstock.com: Hayley Crews (tl). 154 Dorling Kindersley: Alan Murphy (clb, bl). Dreamstime.com: Melvin Ray Herr (c); Mark Hryciw (cla). 155 Dreamstime.com: Charles Brutlag (cra/Tufted); Michael Truchon (cra); Paul Reeves (cra/House Wren). naturepl.com: Alan Murphy / BIA (cb). 156 Alamy Stock Photo: Daybreak Imagery. 158 Dreamstime.com: Dennis Donohue (br); Petar Kremenarov (tl). 159 Dorling Kindersley: Tom Grey (br). Dreamstime.com: Chris Lorenz (tl). 160 Dreamstime.com: Steve Byland (tr); Paul Reeves (bl). 161 Dreamstime.com: Steve Byland (br); Michael Truchon / Mtruchon (tl). 162 Dreamstime.com: Rkpimages (tl); Senorrojo (br). 163 Dreamstime.com: Mikelane45 (br); Teekaygee (tl). 164 Dreamstime.com: Steve Byland (tr); Imogen Warren (tl). 165 Dreamstime.com: Dennis Donohue (br); Vasiliy Vishnevskiy (bl). 166 Dreamstime.com: Jgorzynik (br); Petar Kremenarov (tl). 167 Alamy Stock Photo: All Canada Photos / Nick Saunders (tr); Nature Photographers Ltd / Brian E Small (br). 168 123RF.com: Raymond Hennessy (tr). Dreamstime.com: Steve Byland (bl). 169 Alamy Stock Photo: Nature Photographers Ltd / Brian E Small (br). Dreamstime.com: Llmckinne (tr). 170 Dorling Kindersley: Alan Murphy (br). Dreamstime.com: Ondřej Prosický (tl). 171 Dreamstime.com: Charles Brutlag (br); Trevor Jones (tl). 172 Dreamstime.com: Michael Truchon (tr); Wildphotos (tl). 173 Dreamstime.com: Charles Brutlag (bl); Jnjhuz (br). 174 Dreamstime.com: Charles Brutlag (tl); Gerald Marella (tr). 175 Dreamstime.com: Gerald Marella (bl); Paul Reeves (tr). 176 Dreamstime.com: Rinus Baak (br); Steve Byland (tl). 177 Dreamstime.com: K Quinn Ferris (br); Mark Hryciw (tl). 178 Dreamstime.com: Earnesttse (br); K Quinn Ferris (tl). 179 Dreamstime.com: John Anderson (tr); Linnette Engler (tl). 180 Dreamstime.com: Charles Brutlag (tl); Steve Byland (br). 181 Dreamstime.com: Sue Feldberg (br); Feng Yu (tl). 182 Dreamstime.com: Mark Hryciw (tl); Brian Kushner (tr). 183 Dreamstime.com: Charles Brutlag (bl); Wildphotos (br). 184 Dreamstime.com: 19838623doug (tl); Jarek2313 (br). 185 Alamy Stock Photo: imageBROKER (tl). Dreamstime.com: Denis Dore (br). 192 Dorling Kindersley: Alan Murphy (br)

All other images © Dorling Kindersley
For further information see: www.dkimages.com